WINGS OF NIGHT

WINGS OF NIGHT

The Secret Missions of
Group Captain Charles Pickard,
DSO and two bars, DFC

ALEXANDER HAMILTON

CRÉCY BOOKS

This edition published by Crécy Books Ltd. 1993
First published by William Kimber & Co. Ltd, 1977

© Alexander Hamilton, 1977

ISBN 0 947554 34 3

Printed and bound in Great Britain by
Hartnolls Limited, Bodmin, Cornwall

This book is copyright. No part of it may be reproduced in any form without permission in writing from the publishers except by a reviewer who wishes to quote brief passages in connection with a review written for inclusion in a newspaper, magazine or radio broadcast.

To
DOROTHY AND NICK
*without whose help this book could never
have been written*

Contents

		Page
	Acknowledgements	11
I	Wave to me on take-off	17
II	You're on your own	26
III	Ming	35
IV	Target for Tonight	43
V	Bruneval	57
VI	Tempsford	73
VII	L'Affaire Déricourt	116
VIII	The Mosquito and the Wheelbarrow	129
IX	Pickard of Picardy	142
	Epilogue	190
	Awards: Charles Pickard	197
	Awards: Alan Broadley	199
	Index	201

List of Illustrations

	facing page
'Boy' Pickard with his mother and sisters	32
Seventh birthday	32
Sidney Carlin	33
Pickard with his sister Helena	33
Framlingham College	33
Harrow bomber in flight	64
214 Squadron (*Flight International*)	64
Pickard's Harrow bomber K6993	64
	between pages
Dorothy and Charles Pickard, June 1940	64–5
Pickard with his horses	64–5
311 Squadron (*Imperial War Museum*)	64–5
Officers of 311 Squadron (*Imperial War Museum*)	64–5
311 Squadron's mascot (*Imperial War Museum*)	64–5
	facing page
German radio location station at Bruneval (*Imperial War Museum*)	65
The raid on Bruneval (*Imperial War Museum*)	65
Pickard at the time of the Bruneval raid (*Imperial War Museum*)	80
Troops landing at Bruneval (*Imperial War Museum*)	80
Returning from the raid (*Imperial War Museum*)	80
Pickard with some paratroops after the raid (*Imperial War Museum*)	81
Their Majesties inspecting the paratroops (*Imperial War Museum*)	81
Their Majesties watch a demonstration (*Imperial War Museum*)	81
RAF personnel at Tempsford (*Public Records Office*)	112

The equipment barn and cottages at Tempsford *(Echo and Post)*	112
Air Chief Marshal Sir Basil Embry *(Elliott and Fry)*	113
Farewell Ventura	113
Mosquito B35 TA634 *(Stuart Howe)*	113
'Ming' leading the way	144
Evening departure	144

between pages

F/Lt J A Broadley adjusts Pickard's Mae West *(Imperial War Museum)*	144–45
A model of Amiens prison used for briefing *(Imperial War Museum)*	144–45
Low level attack on Amiens Prison *(Imperial War Museum)*	144–45
Smoke pouring from the prison *(Imperial War Museum)*	144–45
The damaged prison *(Imperial War Museum)*	144–45

facing page

Aerial view of the prison after the raid *(Imperial War Museum)*	145
The scene of the crash near St Gratien	176
Carrying the bodies of Pickard and F/Lt J A Broadley	176
The course taken by 'F for Freddie'	176
Pickard's grave	177
LAC A Sullivan and Marie Yuonne at the grave	177
The annual pilgrimage, seen in 1974	177

Acknowledgements

Research into the life story of Group Captain P. C. Pickard has been a singularly gratifying privilege. Throughout his short, action-packed life, it is patently obvious that this 'blond giant of a Yorkshireman' as he was once described was rarely at peace except when in the air. Pick would have had no quarrel with his headmaster at Framlingham College who noted that he excelled at sport while remaining, classically, at the wrong end. He was less understanding of the British Army later. Their comment that he was 'too dim, and not even a crammer would help!' he found amusing rather than annoying. If the army lost a dim soldier, the Royal Air Force gained a brilliant pilot.

Perhaps his career is best summed up by Air Chief Marshal Sir Basil Embry, KCB, CBE, DSO, DFC, AFC, to whom I am indebted for information, particularly on the Amiens raid. Sir Basil writes . . . 'It is impossible to measure Charles Pickard's loss to the RAF and Britain, but in courage, devotion to duty, fighting spirit and powers of real leadership, he stood out as one of the great airmen of the war and as a shining example of British manhood. I always felt he was part of a character from an earlier Elizabethan age.'

Others to whom I am no less indebted are Air Chief Marshal Sir Lewis Hodges, KCB, CBE, DSO, DFC, ADC, RAF, presently Deputy Commander-in-Chief, Allied Forces Central Europe. As Wing Commander Hodges in May of 1943, Sir Lewis took over the hot seat from Charles Pickard at RAF Tempsford and became responsible for the clandestine flights of agents into and out of France. By December of 1943, Lewis Hodges had his own story to tell.

Air Chief Marshal Sir Neil Wheeler, KCB, CBE, DSO, DFC, AFC, and Charles Pickard trained and flew together in the halcyon days of pre-war. It was an accidental meeting with Sir Neil Wheeler at the RAF Museum, Hendon, which sparked the story.

Major General John Dutton Frost, CB, DSO, MC, of Liphook in Hampshire has been most helpful with news of the Bruneval raid and to this, Major Norton of the Airborne Forces' Museum, Aldershot, added further invaluable information.

From the Royal Air Force Museum itself, Jack Bruce has been at all times encouraging and prodigal of help. Further north, Major Goldsmith of Salisbury Hall and the Mosquito Museum has been responsible for information and much appreciated photographs. Salisbury Hall and the Mosquito Museum at London Colney are very much a lasting tribute to Charles Pickard. The Imperial War Museum has been a most fruitful source of photographs, many of which are reproduced in the book, and acknowledged.

Group Captains Ken Batchelor, Hugh Verity and Peter Vaughan-Fowler, all of whom served from RAF Tempsford, have each contributed much valued anecdotes of the time.

Air Commodore E B Sismore, DSO, DFC, AFC, MBIM, RAF, formerly navigator to Sir Basil Embry and very much involved in the early planning of the Amiens raid.

Mr J H Adams of the Records Office in Portugal Street, London, for his time and unqualified patience.

The Lord Gainford, my good friend Joe, an ex-wartime kindred spirit who shared the same patience with the Records Office.

George B Dick of Edinburgh, one of Charles Pickard's first wireless operators/air gunners in the days of the old Harrow bomber.

Eric Burke of Luton for his painstaking work on Tempsford; photographs, and the poem which is quoted.

John Tyler of Chipping Ongar in Essex, a man with an infinite capacity for getting things done.

Lee Howard, the photographer in the Film Unit Mosquito, which covered the results of the Amiens raid.

Dick Sugden, flying in the second wave as a Squadron Leader with 464 Squadron, RAAF, on the Amiens raid.

A H 'Bunny' Bridger, closely associated with Amiens as Dick Sugden's navigator.

The Rev Donald C Caskie, OBE, MA, author of *The Tartan*

Acknowledgements

Pimpernel to whom countless servicemen, including Lewis Hodges, owe their safe return to England after the fall of Dunkirk. Donald Caskie himself was later to be grateful to the men from the 'Moon Squadrons'.

Jean Overton Fuller, author of *Double Webs* for permission to quote from her work and to the Mirror group of newspapers for permission to quote from an article in the *Sunday Pictorial*.

Richard Law, the Chaplain of Framlingham College, for news of the amusing, if irreverent, 'Sabbath Rodeo' instigated by Charles Pickard.

Mrs Margery Woods and Mrs Nancy Tibbett, Charles Pickard's sisters, contributed much towards the early days and shared in his extraordinary escapades.

Across the channel, the French have been no less generous.

M Henri Moisan, incarcerated in Amiens Prison at the time of the raid and who lived to tell the tale.

Giselle Souhait, as Giselle Cage at the time of Amiens, for her eye witness account of the Mosquito's last moments.

M Laurent Cagnart, now Major of St Gratien, who, with Giselle Souhait was one of the first on the scene of the crash.

Throughout research, help has been unstinted and unqualified. To each and every one, I extend my deepest gratitude.

Finally, without the assistance of the perfect secretary, my wife Muriel, and the genius in photography of my Irish friend, Alan Gray, neither the manuscript nor the photographs would have seen the light of day!

WINGS OF NIGHT

The Secret Missions of Group Captain Charles Pickard, DSO and two bars, DFC

CHAPTER ONE

Wave to Me on Take-off

It is not often that a man becomes a legend in his lifetime, particularly when his lifespan is less than 30 years. Such a man was Percy Charles Pickard.

The youngest of a family of five, three girls and two boys, Pickard was born in Sheffield in 1915 and hated the name of Percy. The family called him 'Boy', in deference to his being the youngest. Before Boy was five years old the family moved to London where his father started a catering business which prospered well, and within a few years had expanded to three enterprises. It was to develop further and later to merge with the Mecca Organisation.

From the earliest years, 'Pick' as he liked to be called showed a great interest in animals – all animals. At his London home the servants' lavatory was located at the bottom of the garden and this provided him with the perfect shelter for his rabbits, mice, white rats, tortoise and even a snake.

Pickard's interest in flying did not start until he was nearly nine. Aircraft appearing irregularly overhead fascinated him. He decided to build his own aircraft. The planning staff for his debut into the world of heavier-than-air machines consisted of his sister Nancy, and himself. Nancy was a little older, but not much, and what the two lacked in knowledge of loading surfaces, thrust and lift, they made up for in sheer unqualified enthusiasm. It was a top secret project and no-one else in the family was in the know – not even his mother from whom he had filched bed sheets to make the covers for the wings and tail-plane.

The undercarriage presented no real problem. The frame and four wheels from an abandoned pram served this purpose well and it was only a matter of building an aircraft body over and around it.

Working after school hours and at week-ends, Pick and his sister fashioned their aircraft until it grew into a fair replica of a flying suitcase. Wooden seats from fruit boxes were nailed on the fuselage, and the wooden wings were covered in white sheets. Pick was impatient for a trial run and outside their home there was a hill which seemed to be the obvious and most natural ground for their test flight. The white clad aircraft was wheeled out of their workshop while their mother rested one Saturday afternoon. They made their way to the top of the hill and Pick decided that Nancy would be his first test pilot. If the aircraft took to the air, Pick didn't want to be there.

Nancy was duly installed in the pilot's seat with Pick ready to push from behind. They knew that the moment of truth would come when they reached maximum speed at the foot of the hill and directly opposite their home. What Nancy was supposed to do then was not quite clear. This exercised her mind quite a bit and she voiced her misgivings to Pick.

'What do I do if it takes off?' she asked.

'Wave to me,' replied Pick, and with that they set off down the hill.

The Pickard Special had some difficulty in keeping straight on the take-off run. One of the front wheels had a definite wobble, and the increasing speed did nothing to improve its stability. By the time they reached the bottom of the hill, with Pick pushing furiously from behind, the wobble was rather more pronounced and Nancy found it impossible to keep to the straight and narrow. The machine swung violently to the left, the front wheel collapsed, and the wings were ripped off against the palings outside the house before collapsing in a heap of broken timber and well torn sheets outside their own door.

Together they discussed the possible cause of failure. Nancy suggested that their undoing was the wobbly wheel and Pick coined the comment which was to remain with him throughout his life . . . 'There's always a bloody something!'

For the time being, their aeronautical activities came to an end and Mrs Pickard had to buy new sheets.

It is difficult to say when 'Boy' Pickard first cast his thoughts towards horses, but certainly by the age of twelve he felt himself sufficiently proficient in riding to attempt the art of riding without bridle or saddle. He and his sister Nancy were once cycling in the country, accompanied by three friends. Passing a field where ponies grazed, the group called a halt to make friends with the animal. The ponies seemed reasonably friendly and the field was hidden from the owner's home by the tall and leafy trees. The temptation to ride without permission, saddle or bridle, was too great and Pick selected one with a lean and hungry look to allow him to grip tightly with his legs. Without another thought, he threw his leg over the pony, grabbed it by the mane, and dug his heels into its sides. A more experienced judge of horse-flesh would have noticed from the animal's eye that it had a *mean* and hungry look. It took off, running like a scalded cat. Pick held on grimly, savouring the excitement to the full, and disappeared from view of the others over a rise in the ground.

'He'll be back,' Nancy assured their friends and as Nancy was the oldest of the group and his sister, they bowed to her superior knowledge. They did not have long to wait. The pony made off to the furthest corner of the field with Pick holding on for dear life. When it reached the fence, the pony swerved violently to follow the line of the fence. The move had been anticipated by Pick as he gripped more tightly and leaned towards the centre of the turn. He was still aboard when the animal straightened up and raced for the top of the field. Gripping tightly and leaning inwards, Pick was still in charge, or as much in charge as anyone can ever be of a runaway horse without a saddle or a bridle.

It seemed that the animal did not have the wit to try and buck Pick off. It was saving that for later. The waiting group shortly saw the pony, still going flat out with Pick leaning low over its neck, racing towards them. With little time in hand all the youngsters bolted to the safety of the nearby fence. The other ponies remained standing where Pick's friends had deserted them so suddenly, oblivious to the mean one bearing down upon them at speed. From behind the fence, Pick's friends looked round in time to see a rather demented pony travelling at full speed suddenly throw a buck as it approached the others and, at the same time, stick its toes into the ground in a vicious stop. The last view they had of Pick before he hit the ground was of a small body in a crouched position flying upwards and over the other horses. It was a fine example of free flight.

Less concerned with the beauties of free flight and unrestricted forward movement was 'Boy' Pickard. He hit the ground with a thud and went out like a light. The unconscious aspiring Lester Piggott was carried gently from the field and propped up, still unconscious, on his bicycle. Between them, his friends wheeled him off to the nearest house, which was occupied by the owner of the badly schooled pony, the mean one.

'What a pony! What a ride! What happened?' were his first coherent words.

Charles Pickard became a boarding pupil at Framlingham College, but it did little to increase his academic store of knowledge. As long as there were cricket, rugby, shooting for Garrett House and riding, Pythagoras could wait. The base of a triangle was no substitute for a good run on the rugby ground or a crack at a cricket ball. In all sports he excelled, perhaps significantly in shooting, where he gained an exceptional rating.

He cared little for mathematics and less for the classics and earned the doubtful distinction of being bottom of the class with a regularity which did not embarrass him in the least. He was quite sure that the only way to get him out of school would be to burn the place down.

The present second master at Framlingham College, Mr N F Barrett, was a contemporary of Charles Pickard and recalls him as a member of the 2nd XV at rugby, not especially bright, but full of fun. The school ran a play in which the boys had to perform before Pick's sister, Helena, who was an actress. In front of such a distinguished guest, the pupils were nervous and the play was a monumental flop.

It would seem that the accident and subsequent concussion from riding the pony bareback and without a bridle in the field a few years earlier had not taught Pick a lesson. Sundays were devoted to church in the morning and the riding of Mr Robinson's cows in the fields at the back of the college in the afternoon, as 'the Sabbath Rodeo' at which Pick excelled. Less impressed was Mr Robinson who could not account for the sudden drop in milk on a Monday morning. It is recorded in the *Framlinghamian* of 1932 that the champion rider in the 'Sabbath Rodeo' also won the house shooting competition for Garrett House. The prowess displayed as a rider and a shot indicated at a fairly early age that Pick, war apart, would make a first class cowboy. The activities certainly appealed to him much more than his persecutor Pythagoras. The indifference with which he accepted his low academic status was not one of disrespect to his learned masters or brighter contemporaries. It was an early indication of his ability to recognise his limitations, and concentrate on his natural assets which belonged, not in a classroom, but to the great outdoors. Disappointing though his school reports may have been, Pick was to retain and cherish an affection for his old school at Framlingham throughout his life.

At the age of seventeen his immediate future was resolved. One of his contemporaries at Framlingham had been invited by his father in Kenya to make his way to East Africa and join him on the farm. The son of the farmer in Kenya was also invited to bring a friend for company. He mentioned the idea to Pick and nothing, at that time, could have been more welcome, or a greater challenge. He accepted with alacrity.

Together the two lads reached Mombasa and from there made their way up country. It was another world of sunshine, vast open spaces, and teeming with wild life. The farm extended to 5,000 acres of undulating country, fertile, and the rains in Kenya allowed two crops to be grown each year. After England, it was all so vast and warm. Animals in abundance to satisfy his first love and unlimited riding each day as they checked on the animals and the crops. The next four years were to be among the happiest of his life. His young friend from England fell by the wayside and returned to England within the year. Pick stayed on, never more happy than when riding across country on a warm and pleasant day.

The remote life had its compensations. Their nearest neighbour was a few miles distant and social activities were confined to week-ends at the local country club. With horses being freely available on the farms, polo was the easiest and most natural game for the farmers and their assistants to play. The annual agricultural shows were the highlight of the farming year with show-jumping competitions and 'best trained polo pony' events, in all of which Pick took part. He became known as a fearless rider, with very good hands, a quality to be found in the best of pilots.

Being a natural ball player, and with a feeling and understanding for horses, Pick was introduced to polo by a certain Sidney Carlin who was universally known as 'Timbertoes' for the simple reason that he had a wooden leg.

Timbertoes Carlin had been a pilot with No 74 Squadron, Royal Flying Corps, flying SE 5a's in the First World War. He was credited with a personal score of 37 enemy aircraft and, by the end of the war had an MC DFC and a DCM. He lost his leg in a flying accident. He was short, extremely active, and always appeared to be in a hurry. This remarkable pace at which he moved had earned him the title of Twinkletoes. With the loss of his leg and the addition of a wooden replacement, the title was altered to Timbertoes. He was now in Kenya, managing a farm for a German baron, and Timbertoes could outride the best of them across country. There was always a side bet at stake and Sidney Carlin rarely lost. He took a particular liking for the tall youngster who had recently arrived from England and determined to show Pick all the shots of polo from a wooden horse.

True to type, Timbertoes challenged the neighbouring farmers to organise their own polo team with a combined handicap of not more than six. In his own team, out of the four players Timbertoes rated a three handicap with the others not yet handicapped. All were young, with the exception of their leader, and he knew that all could ride and strike the ball with confidence. The team was known as the 'Timberlings'. Timbertoes Carlin was ready to take the field.

Within two years, under the able and experienced tuition of his good friend Timbertoes Carlin, Charles Pickard was to rate a three handicap at polo and played in the annual tournaments. Kenya introduced him seriously to a disease known as 'horse in the blood', from which he never quite recovered. By the same token, the fast and exciting game of polo had taught him a salutary lesson. Success springs from doing your homework, lots of practice, and obeying the rules. It was a lesson he was never to forget, imprinted in his mind by the glorious feeling of scoring his first goal on the polo field.

The four years in Kenya were to pass all too quickly. By 1936 it became patently clear to Charles Pickard that war was inevitable, with Hitler and the Nazis riding roughshod over Europe. He had no intention of being left out in the heat, and he decided to return to Britain to join one of the services. With his three young friends from the Timberlings polo team, who were of the same mind, they bought an old car between them for £50, and decided to drive overland to England.

The quartet set out from Kenya heading north in the general direction of England. It was a gruelling trip in a car of pre-1936 vintage which seemed to excel in collecting dust on the ill-made roads and in some places mere patches of scrub and desert. The old car kept chugging along faithfully as the uplands of Central Africa gave way to the more inhospitable north and their first real serious onset of trouble in the Nile Delta. Travelling overland, camping under the stars, and constantly plagued by mosquitoes, Charles Pickard went down with a severe bout of malaria. For a matter of ten days he suffered unbearable headaches; the party could not move on, and for some time he lay unconscious.

His condition deteriorated until he became completely comatose with a pulse beat which was barely perceptible. There was little anyone could do except try to administer as much quinine as they could slip down his throat. On the eleventh day they awakened to hear his breathing a degree louder and more regular. Later in the day his eyes opened and his first request was for a glass of water, with ice. Recovering from a severe bout of malaria and the effects of dehydration, he found the cool water worked miracles. The first glass had a teaspoonful of salt added to it to counteract the effects of dehydration and the saline solution caused no nausea. Apart from the effects of malaria, his body was crying out for salt. The second glass he sipped more slowly as strength almost visibly returned to his body.

The hard farming, walking and riding life in Kenya, had turned his body into whipcord and it was this, more than anything else, which had carried him through the bout of malaria.

The passage across the Mediterranean was bliss in comparison. After the dust, heat, insects and mosquitoes of the arid desert regions of Africa, the cool waters of the Mediterranean and the cleanliness of a proper bed gave the quartet their first glimpse of civilised luxury for months. With the resilience of youth, Charles Pickard shed the debilitating effects of his malaria as the ship plodded on towards Marseilles and his first view of Europe in four years. The old port of Marseilles was spread lazily before them in the early morning haze.

The trip north through France followed a course with which Pick was later to become closely acquainted. The resources of the intrepid four began to reach harrowingly low proportions as funds had to be conserved to meet the cost of the crossing of the English Channel. Their arrival in France coincided with the grape harvest and their diet was largely augmented by very large, juicy grapes filched from the nearby vineyards. Their luck, the car, and their resources held out until they reached the environs of London itself. By then, old Henry Ford was feeling very sorry for himself. The grinding dust of North Africa at last took its toll, the two rear wheels made ominous sounds and, without further warning, both collapsed. Together they piled out, removed their belongings and lifted Henry Ford gently into the side of the road. The car which had brought them safely overland from Kenya in Central Africa found its last resting place beside the tramlines in outer London.

Each decided to make his separate way home and, in the small hours of the morning, Pick found a taxi to take him across London. The taxi arrived at his home at 3 o'clock in the morning. One final problem still remained – he did not have enough money for his taxi fare! He asked the driver to wait while he knocked on the door of his home. After much banging and thumping on the door, he could hear movement inside and a light appeared in the hallway and the living room. Outside the door stood the tall, dishevelled and unshaven figure of Percy Charles Pickard. The door was opened by his mother who had not heard from Pick for months and believed that he was still in Kenya. His frame was outlined against the dark background by the hallway light. Mrs Pickard, aroused from the sleep of the just at 3 am, was in no way prepared for further shocks. She took one look at her son and, as quickly, fainted!

It was not Charles Pickard's nature to rest up or relax for long. A war was inevitable and the sooner he became organised for the drama ahead, the happier he would be. He applied at the local army headquarters to become a soldier. His application was quickly accepted and he was asked to attend a protracted interview for training as an officer. The interview resulted in his being subjected to a further session of tests, examinations, mathematical problems on paper and the whole gamut of tricks designed by the army to ascertain the best possible officer material. In these he failed, causing him to comment later that the Army had reported that he was 'too dim, and not even a crammer would help!' The Army has been known to make mistakes.

His next alternative was the flying branch of the Royal Air Force. The pre-war 'aptitude' tests of the RAF were both involved and stringent. Basically, one had to be medically fit and mentally alert.

Planned over the years with a great deal of experience from which the RAF could draw, going back to the string and wire days of the Royal Flying Corps, Percy Charles Pickard passed the examination board's extensive tests with surprising ease and, from that day on, had found his niche. It seemed that he had a natural aptitude for flying.

In November 1936 he was posted to the Airwork Reserve Flying Training School at Perth in Scotland. The fledgling was about to gain its wings.

CHAPTER TWO

You're on your own

Pickard's flying training began in a Tiger Moth at Perth in November of 1936. Scotland in wintertime has a raw and bitterly cold wind which sweeps across the moorlands to test the tough on the ground and makes conditions well nigh impossible in the air. Tiger Moths were not fitted with all mod cons, and there was no heating in their cockpits. Flights were restricted to days when an inkling of sky could be seen through the clouds. The month of November offered a total of nine hours when these relatively ideal conditions could be found. In his first month of flying, Charles Pickard logged nine hours, a gross total which he would frequently exceed later in one flight. The rest of the time was spent trying to get the aircraft started.

It is the greatest ambition of all pilots under training to be taken up by a different instructor as this generally signifies a 'solo check', and heralds a culminating point in the life of an embryo pilot, going solo. It is a very thrilling moment of which memories are made. After ten hours and ten minutes of dual instruction, Pick was on his own. He went solo on a day when the weather-man relented, and the first big hurdle had been cleared. The new instructor who had checked him out asked him to complete two circuits and landings. These were completed according to the book, and they taxied back to the point of take-off. The instructor climbed out of the aircraft with his parachute, tightened the straps in the seat, and leaned into the machine to speak to Pick against the noise of the engine.

'Right, son,' he began, 'you're on your own. Take her up, do one circuit, come in and land, and try to make the landing in one piece.'

He walked away and stood at the end of the runway. Vital action take-off drill, trim more nose-down to counteract the loss of weight of the instructor, keep straight on take-off, and finger out. Pick was ready for take-off, and he opened the throttle steadily and firmly, holding it tight in his hand. The light aircraft, notably more responsive now that the instructor had gone, gathered speed quickly. The tail came up, he held the machine straight with quite a pressure on the rudder bar, and before he knew it, he had reached flying speed. He eased back on the control column and there was an instant, light and superb feeling of buoyancy. He was airborne, and on his own.

Throughout the climb to 300 feet, then the climbing turn to the left, he was conscious of nothing except remembering everything he had been taught. At 1,200 feet he levelled off, throttled back to cruising revs and prepared to turn left to the downwind leg. A gentle turn, keep her straight, and hold the airfield on the end of the port wing. For the very first time he enjoyed the complete realisation that he was flying solo as he relaxed on the downwind leg and noticed the empty cockpit ahead. It came home to him with such glorious finality that, instead of holding the aircraft straight and level, he eased the control column back and forward, making the aircraft rise up and down. He did this just to convince himself that he was really in charge. The aircraft responded with the lightness of a feather and he was enjoying the thrill of 'me over matter' so much that he overshot his turn to the left at the end of the airfield by a fraction and a fraction can be a long time on your first solo.

Pulling himself together, he swung the aircraft to port, throttled back and began his descent. At 500 feet he turned into wind and lined up with the centre of the airfield. His angle of descent indicated an undershoot as a result of playing cowboys on the downwind leg, and he opened the throttle to carry him well clear of the boundary. Steady as you go, he cleared the boundary, cut the throttle and settled down to hold off, wait for the controls to become sluggish, then ease back on the stick.

The machine seemed to stay airborne for so much longer now that he was on his own and any tendency to bring the control column back too soon met with a rise in height from the ground. Holding it steady for what seemed ages, he gradually started to ease back and found the aircraft had lost its desire to rise and the controls became very sluggish. He eased back further into the three point attitude, kept straight with the rudder bar, and waited. Like the snowflakes which began to fall around him, the aircraft settled with never a jolt.

It was a great improvement on his efforts with his sister Nancy in the home-made Pickard Special.

By mid January 1937, Charles Pickard survived all the hazards of Elementary Flying Training School, aerobatics, and cross countries, and was assessed simply as 'Average'. He had a total of 53 flying hours and had not bent a single aircraft. He was on his way.

Ten days at Uxbridge followed before Pick was posted to RAF Wittering and No 11 FTS. The aircraft used at this time for advanced training were Harts and their sister aircraft, the Audax. The full complement of elementary and advanced exercises on Harts and the Audax was continued without respite until May of 1937 when Pupil Pilot Percy Pickard became Acting Pilot Officer PC Pickard and was awarded the flying badge with effect from 22nd May 1937. His total flying hours now reached 120 and Pick had cleared his second hurdle.

It is a significant reflection on the extent and thorough grounding of the peace time air force that, within the year, Charles Pickard had completed 345 flying hours in seventeen different types of aircraft, from single engine elementary trainers to the twin engined Harrow bomber. His assessment as a pilot was now 'Above the Average'. From this era, one of Pick's first wireless operators/air gunners, George Dick, remembers Pick as having an uncanny knack at navigation, and this asset, added to his rating as an 'Above Average' pilot was to stand Pick in good stead during the desperate years.

Dorothy Hodgkin and her sister Hilary were born into a family of the old military school. Their father, Harry Sidney Hodgkin, was a Lieutenant Colonel in the 1st Cheshire Regiment and their mother, Elsie Gray McMordie, was the daughter of the Lord Mayor of Belfast. Their marriage had caused considerable stir in Ireland as it was to be solemnised in the Belfast Assembly Hall. It was by far the wedding of the year in Belfast and the ceremony was one of the most brilliant in the social life of the country.

Dorothy and Hilary were in 1937 living close to the Central Flying Training School at Wittering. The monotony of life in the mess at Wittering was occasionally broken by holding a mess dance, to which suitable young ladies in the neighbourhood would be invited. To one such dance, both Dorothy and her sister Hilary were invited. They found it rather dreary and boring. The music for the evening was provided by a gramophone for dancing which scratched out a few of the latest hits, the mess was bare of furniture and empty of guests, and by nine in the evening, both girls had made up their minds that there would be more activity in front of the fire with a good book. Of the two, Hilary was the more reluctant to leave. She sensed that their early departure might be interpreted as rudeness and she did not wish to cause offence. She suggested that they should bear it out for just a little longer in the hope that something would happen.

Dorothy agreed and continued to sit, quite convinced that it was a complete waste of time.

Her thoughts of home, book and fireside, suddenly evaporated at the sight of a young, tall and very handsome man standing in front of her. He bowed, and quietly asked Dorothy if she would care to dance. The music being played was a tango, and ironically, was called 'Don't Play with Fire!' Her partner was dressed in his best mess kit with a stripe down the side of his trouser leg and looked very distinguished.

'You must be at least a flight lieutenant', Dorothy began in her opening gambit of conversation, being none too familiar with the badges of rank in the Royal Air Force.

'Me?' laughed her partner with obvious amusement, 'no, I am nothing so high and mighty. I am Pupil Pilot Percy Pickard!'

His very friendly manner and quick sense of humour appealed at once to Dorothy and the evening perked up considerably. It was in the very late hours that Hilary managed to persuade Dorothy to make tracks for home.

The tall young gentleman of the previous evening was never one to allow grass to grow under his feet. He called by telephone the following day to ask Dorothy to accompany him to the motor racing at Donnington where John Cobb was racing. The invitation she was only too ready to accept, but Dorothy shrank at the thought of asking her father if she could go out for the day with a strange young man whom she had met at a dance. All her previous escorts had to be introduced and vetted to make certain that they were suitable. Afraid that Pupil Pilot Percy Pickard might not pass muster, Dorothy wrote a short note for her father, and fled the house. It was a glorious day and Dorothy thoroughly enjoyed herself despite the thought of facing her father in the evening. They returned from Donnington in a most extraordinary chain-driven Kleino car which had the doors tied with pieces of elastic. With a rattle and a shake they arrived at the Hodgkin homestead, to an aloof and stony welcome. The chain-driven Kleino was regarded with a positively jaundiced look and the rubber bands did not help.

Charles Pickard was not invited into the house. With as much fortitude as he could muster but in obvious embarrassment, he returned to his dejected Kleino which slowly coughed into life, and he drove off at a rattling good pace. A thick belch of acrid exhaust fumes hung in the cold night air.

In no uncertain terms, Dorothy was told that her companion was considered unsuitable either as a suitor or as a boy-friend, that he was the very personification of the rake's progress, that his intentions were neither honourable nor in keeping with the conduct of an officer and a gentleman, and please would she take care that she never saw him again.

It was a rather splendid tirade against someone her father had never met, knew nothing about, nor was he prepared to listen to reason. Dorothy was twenty-four, and she decided to pack her bags. Her main possession was a racehorse called 'Marie José' after the Belgian Crown Princess. The mare was being trained at Northolt Racecourse and was due to run at Northolt on the Easter Monday. It seemed as good a time as any to shake the dust of home from her feet. She packed her suitcase and called on her mother in the kitchen who was busy giving instructions to the cook. Without any preamble Dorothy said to her mother, 'Goodbye, I am leaving!'

Her mother was taken aback and replied, 'Don't be silly, you can't leave.'

Steeling herself, Dorothy said firmly to her mother, 'I can cope and I'm going. Goodbye.'

The precious little amount of money she had in her purse was too valuable to squander on the doubtful outcome of a horse race, but her horse was considerate enough to win and from this the trainer was able to add a little to her kitty.

In London, the prospects were bleak indeed. The sheltered life had left her ill-equipped to handle a typewriter, or book-keeping, and this serious omission in her earlier training would have to be put right.

In London she managed to contact the sister of an old boy-friend who was a submarine commander. He, too, had failed to make the grade with her father. She also managed to borrow a typewriter which appeared to have been trampled in the ark by the animals. Shortly after, Dorothy rented her own bed-sitter at 32/6d a week and ate in a little cafe round the corner where a very reasonable meal could be bought for tenpence. It was a lonely, friendless and penny-pinching existence, with no hope of earning an income until she had learned to master the temperamental and prehistoric typewriter.

Out of the blue came a loud knock on the door. She opened the door to her tall, handsome Royal Air Force friend, now wearing the thin blue line of a pilot officer.

'What the hell are you doing here?' began Charles Pickard as he bustled into the room.

'Well,' Dorothy replied, 'I ran away from home because you were not satisfactory and none of my other gentlemen admirers seemed to be able to measure up. None of the friends I choose have an unearned income of four thousand pounds a year, or a title, so they are out'.

Pick in his easiest and most disarming manner wasted no words.

'How are you coping?'

'Not very well,' answered Dorothy truthfully.

'Look,' continued Pick, 'my sister is looking for someone to do her typing and manage the house, look after the entertainment of her guests, arrange flowers and take the child to school.'

Dorothy thought for a moment, but not a long moment.

'Splendid,' she replied, 'as long as there is not too much typing I can cope with most things.'

From her 32/6d bed-sitter off Baker Street, Dorothy went daily to the beautiful home in Avenue Road. It was the London home of Pick's elder sister Helena who was by now married to Sir Cedric Hardwicke, the actor.

The boredom and loneliness of the bed-sitter was soon replaced by a succession of endless parties, generally given in honour of visiting American film directors. Of these, one had the unnerving compulsion of running around the corridors stark naked chasing maids who took no notice and were much more fleet of foot. Dorothy's first introduction to the odd antics of the man caused her to drop a large vase of flowers she was placing in the hallway as a laughing, giggling servant sped past with the naked apparition in hot pursuit. The days of her sheltered life were shattered.

The hectic and oft hilarious days which involved hard work and long hours came to an end when Helena left England to join Sir Cedric in America. The friends and the contacts from the Hardwicke home in Avenue Road made it easier for Dorothy to find suitable employment and she moved to a beauty shop in Berkely Square. Her parents had now become reconciled to the fact that she was now earning her own living and she was invited back home. During the summer Pick and Dorothy became engaged and this great event was celebrated at Avenue Road in typical Avenue Road fashion, but it was an event which Dorothy did not feel disposed to discuss with her uncompromising parents.

Dorothy moved down to Budley in Devonshire to her grandmother's house, contracted meningitis, and was confined to the Cottage Hospital. Pick had been posted to RAF Cranwell as ADC to Air Marshal Jackie Baldwin but managed to keep in touch with Dorothy by writing to her every day. The crisis passed and Dorothy was able to drive to Cranwell, stay with friends, and see Pick as much as possible.

The summer of 1939 passed, and with it all hope of peace in Europe. At the outbreak of war on 3rd September, Dorothy decided to leave home for good, travel to London and join the London Ambulance Volunteer Service. The vehicle which Dorothy was given to drive was a Swan Laundry van with a gear lever extending to her left armpit, making life and manoeuvring both difficult. Pick was never very far away and one day he bounced into the emergency ambulance building.

'Look here, we are going to get married. Wives are not allowed to live on the station, but it is time to get married!'

The Registry Office at Caxton Hall in the district of the City of Westminster was a far cry from the crowded opulence at the wedding of Dorothy's parents in the Belfast Assembly Hall. Pick and Dorothy were not going to be troubled with crowds, and not even her own parents were among the select six who attended. Dorothy was afraid that her father might not approve. The simple ceremony was interrupted for two minutes' silence. It was the eleventh hour of the eleventh month, 1939.

The wedding ceremony in Caxton Hall was followed by a luncheon party at the Savoy Hotel. One of Pick's sisters, Marjorie,

(Right) 'Boy' Pickard with his mother and sisters, Nancy (standing) and Helena.

(Below) Seventh birthday, with the lastest addition to the zoo.

The irrepressible Sidney 'Timbertoes' Carlin, the man with RFC Pilot's wings and the RAF air gunner's brevet.

'Pupil Pilot Percy Pickard' with his actress sister Helena who married Sir Cedric Hardwicke.

Framlingham College, scene of the 'Sabbath Rodeos'.

had offered to give them a reception party in the evening, and in the afternoon they went to a film show suitably entitled *The Lion Roars*. The real luxury of their wedding and honeymoon was spent in a suite at the Hyde Park Hotel, where the phone rang every ten minutes throughout the evening and night from a roster set up by Pick's pilot friends at Upper Heyford. Pick's patience was sorely tried.

In the morning, Pick had to return to his squadron at Upper Heyford and Dorothy returned to her ambulance driving. The wedding and the honeymoon had lasted one whole day.

On leaving, Pick gave Dorothy £20 and asked her to buy a car he had seen. It was a very tiny Fiat. It was the fashion at the time for ladies to wear hats, decorated with a feather, and the longer the more fashionable. Fortunately the Fiat had a sunshine roof and it had to be opened to allow Dorothy to drive wearing her hat. The other problem was Pick's height. Six feet four of Charles Pickard driving along the road in their minute Fiat would require the sunshine roof to be left open in all weathers. The Fiat, in Dorothy's opinion, was definitely a non-starter, but she had to admit that it was an improvement on his chain-driven Kleino and it smoked a lot less.

Back at the ambulance station, two of the driving instructors were both taxi drivers and knew a great deal about changing wheels, changing oil, changing gears and running repairs. Dorothy felt that their knowledge might easily extend to changing cars. Please, could they help her to find a reliable car for £20? One of the instructors, by the nickname of 'Zulu' came back with a Ford 8 in practically new condition. The rickety chain-driven Kleino had gone like a bomb, with much the same noise. The Ford 8 positively sparkled in the sun and the inside was 'indistinguishable from new' as the dealers would have them believe. In the event, Dorothy set course for Upper Heyford in the Ford 8 in place of the tiny Fiat, not entirely sure of Pick's reaction to her change of plan. But the car travelled without a murmur and Pick was delighted at the shiny new Ford 8. After the Kleino, it was the last thing in opulence.

The Royal Air Force began to relax on its rule which forbade wives on air stations and shortly after the arrival of the opulent car, Dorothy was able to join Pick. He had found a delightful house which had belonged to Sir John Simon's mother at the time when Sir John Simon was Minister of Air. They moved into a very modern, beautifully furnished home with cherry blossom trees on either side of the path leading to the house. They were very happy and the world was their oyster.

Inevitably, it was time to move to another posting and Pick was sent to Stormy Down in Wales within the vicinity of Porthcawl. They managed to find accommodation in a small hotel near Porthcawl at £7 a week for both of them. Reasonable though this may seem, Pick's salary was £25 a month, and this left them with a shortfall of £3. They were feeling the effects of being financially embarrassed, and the Grand National was due to be run. With horse-in-the-blood, Dorothy decided to have a flutter on 'Bogscar', belonging to Lord Stallbridge.

'I am going to back this horse', Dorothy announced to Pick.

'You're bloody mad!' Pick answered, and left it at that.

In Porthcawl, Dorothy found herself a bookie and lashed out with her last £2. Bogscar drew away from the field, and won. The winnings replenished Dorothy's piggy bank and paid their hotel bill for a month.

CHAPTER THREE

Ming

The Royal Air Force had no illusions about the conflict ahead and the protestations of Adolf Hitler that all he sought was peace in Europe fell on deaf ears and frantic behind the scenes activity by those among the higher hierarchy in the most junior service. By the outbreak of war in September 1939, Pick had a total of 776 flying hours in a remarkable number of 32 different types of aircraft. The earlier observation of George Dick was apparent to the authorities. As a pilot and as a pilot-navigator, Charles Pickard was now assessed as 'Above Average' in both categories. He was ready, willing and able for war. He was not to be found wanting.

At the beginning of war, Britain was still to suffer from the misplaced belief by the politicians in that Hitler's intentions were non-aggressive. With the German armies marching unchecked through Europe, this was a sad and tragic assessment of the aims of the Third Reich. On 3rd September 1939, there was little to suggest a successful confrontation with the might of the German war machine which had been building up for several years prior to the declaration of war made by Britain. In men, ships, guns and aircraft, Britain was sadly lacking.

The Local Defence Volunteers, later to become the Home Guard and made up of the under-aged and the over-aged for active service, trained with pitchforks instead of guns. In the country and in the hills, farmers and farmers' sons patrolled the open country with tractors by night and, if they were lucky, had a shot gun with which to repel the expected invaders from the sky. Silently, grimly, and to a man, each had a part to play with no light on the horizon to relieve the gloom.

On leave for a few days, Charles Pickard was of a mind to visit one of his old friends who was now in charge of the Home Guard in

Chertsey, Surrey. His friend had been an officer in the First World War and was now commander of the Chertsey Home Guard. Trained in the trenches, he was a stickler for discipline, and was at pains to explain to Pick the disposition of his various units, and the reasons. It was an impressive explanation. He invited Pick to accompany him on one of his routine night rounds, particularly to see his top-flight, hand-picked unit on guard in the tower of the old Chertsey Church. He explained how his men in the Chertsey Church had spent the late afternoon and evening painting pikes a brilliant red 'as this was the only colour available'. They were now in the church tower awaiting the arrival of the Germans, with their red pikes.

Walking through the deserted and frozen streets, they set out for the church. The windows of houses were totally blacked out and finding their way was more by instinct than good navigation. The night was particularly black and silent.

Nearing Chertsey Church, they were greeted by a strange sound. The strains of the organ could be heard breaking the complete silence of the night. For a moment they listened, believing that the church organist might be rehearsing for the Sunday service. The music drifting out to them could hardly be called sacred. Hastening to the door, they opened and closed it quickly. Seated at the organ, dressed in the black robes of the Vicar, one of the Chertsey Home Guard was belting out 'In the Mood'. Around him, also in the Holy cloth of the Vicar, the other members of this private platoon pranced in time to the music, in the eerie light of a single candle.

The approach of the guard commander was a signal for the Joe Loss and his band of Chertsey Church to call a halt.

'What the hell is going on?' spat out Pick's friend.

'Nothing, Sir,' came the answer. 'We were frozen stiff up the tower, needed clothes and a bit of action!'

'You are all on a charge,' blurted out the seething commander, 'the Germans could be here any minute and all you can think of doing is dress up for a Halloween party and play "In the Mood"!'

Suitably penitent, the Chertsey Home Guard stumbled upstairs to the tower in the dark to await the penalty for their misdeeds. It was not long in coming. To a man they were given a further dozen pikes to paint.

The German Armies had marched with barely a check through the countries over which Hitler had designs. In a speech in the House of Commons on 11th April 1940, Winston Churchill made clear the intolerable disadvantage which the Allies had suffered during the seven months of war by the free use of Norwegian territorial waters, permitted to all manner of Geman shipping. He explained how the peculiar configuration of the Norwegian coastline provided a kind of corridor or 'covered way' through which German ships could move without being molested.

The proposal was made to the Norwegian authorities that a minefield should be laid, a proposal which had been agreed to in the First World War but which was now emphatically rejected. This rejection placed the British Government in an invidious position. Either Britain would have to recognise a status quo which was becoming unbearable, or to reluctantly disregard the principles of International Law for which they were fighting.

As it turned out, during the last week in March the Germans were using the Norwegian corridor to send empty ore ships forward with military stores and concealed troops. When the moment was ripe for the swoop by the Germans on the Norwegian ports which they desired to make their own, supplies and men would be available on the spot. Once again Hitler was one jump ahead. When the British minefields were laid, the invasion of Norway had already begun, according to plans laid down and in process of fulfilment for at least a month before. Later evidence showed that several years earlier Germany had carried out purposeful surveys of Scandinavian waters.

The invasion of Norway on 8th April had been preceded by a continued and ruthless attack on her shipping while she could still claim the right of a neutral power. Norway was in not state to withstand the well planned and quickly executed forces of evil from Germany and her resistance at this time was no more than token.

Across the water in the tight little island Charles Pickard had teamed up with Sergeant J A Broadley as his navigator at this time and their first operations together were directed against German shipping in Norway. This partnership was the beginning of a unique and successful example of team work which was later to be described as the 'war's greatest air partnership'. Both were with

No 99 Squadron flying Wellingtons from Newmarket and Pick was now a fully fledged flying officer with 950 hours to his credit. For the last week in April they became acquainted in their assaults on shipping in Norway, but Norway could not hold out for long and by 2nd May the Allied Forces were being evacuated. With the impudence of David against Goliath, the embryo force of Bomber Command turned its attention to Germany, Belgium and the Low Countries.

In June of 1940, No 99 Squadron was stationed at Newmarket Racecourse. Racing being out of fashion 'for the duration' Pick managed to acquire two thoroughbred horses at Newmarket.

When off duty, Dorothy and Pick would ride over Newmarket Heath closely followed by Ming, Dorothy's English sheep dog, in the early morning. It was a profound relief from the tension of operational flying and these rides became regular rabbit hunts. Cantering along the undulating English countryside with Ming loping along close behind, Pick would spot a warren of rabbits, whistle loudly with his fingers in his mouth, and Ming raced up, followed the direction in which Pick threw his arm, cleared the hedge, and chased after the unsuspecting rabbits. It was all great fun, and, with the intelligence for which sheep dogs are famous, Ming became an expert and a highly successful rabbit hunter.

Between rabbit hunting in the early morning and cross country flights over England when her Master was carrying out exercises, Ming acquired a nose for rabbits, her own flying log book, and an understanding with Pick which became uncanny. It was an understanding of his moods, his triumphs and disasters, which was a psychic phenomenon.

Of this Dorothy had an early indication when operations over enemy territory began in earnest. At first Dorothy felt that Ming was simply pining in her own way for Pick. The great English sheep dog would remain restless after Pick took off on a raid. With successive flights, Dorothy noticed that Ming did not remain restless throughout the flight. Somewhere between take-off and landing Ming would cease to be restless, lie down, and go to sleep.

The full significance of this did not become apparent until 19th June 1940.

In Wellington N 3200, 'O for Orange', with Pick at the controls and Alan Broadley now becoming firmly established as his navigator, they set off for a target, bombing a factory east of the Ruhr. The crew complement was made up of three other members, Sergeants Mills, Hanigan and Harniman. The total number of aircraft involved was six, each carrying eight 250 pound bombs, two 500 pound bombs and one container of incendiaries. The intention was to open the factory at the seams, then set it alight for good measure. With plans well laid, morale high, and Ming to see them off, they set course for the Ruhr.

Against fierce opposition from ground fire, they pressed home their attack shortly after midnight, evading the flak as best they could. 'O for Orange' received enough damage to the starboard engine to put it out of action. They turned for home on one engine, labouring under the strain of high revs, in an effort to clear the target area. Heading towards the North Sea, and home, the oil pressure began to drop alarmingly in the port engine and height began to be lost. Pick nursed the aircraft in an effort to place as much distance between themselves and the enemy coastline as possible.

Beneath them lay the cold and dark waters of the North Sea, never an inviting prospect, but with a swim coming up shortly after three o'clock in the morning, perish the thought. Watching the altimeter closely and staying on track to facilitate an air search for his aircraft and crew later, Pick and Alan Broadley peered into the darkness to catch sight of anything that looked like water.

'Ditching stations!' Pick called to his crew as the white horses began to emerge.

Bracing themselves for the impact, still with the utmost faith in their skipper, the crew waited.

The sea has a very arresting effect on aircraft which are not designed for such a manoeuvre and 'O for Orange' was no exception. With the water now clearly visible and very little height left in hand, Pick cut his ailing port engine and held the aircraft off as long as possible to reduce flying speed. His aim was to hit the water when the aircraft reached the point of stall, thereby reducing the force of the impact. The irresticle was about to meet the immovable.

The crew had tightened their safety belts and were braced against the inevitable scrunch.

'O for Orange' met the North Sea breakers with the full grace and dignity of a brick. The rough sea tore at the belly of the aircraft, and, even with straps fully tightened, Pick's massive frame was thrown violently against the instrument panel, damaging his wrist and breaking his watch.

When the aircraft settled, no time was lost in getting outside and all hands helping to release the dinghy. The dinghy was expected to be self-releasing when an aircraft hit water, but in the cold, the wet and the dark, the crew were taking no chances. For the first time that night they were lucky. The dinghy floated. They clambered aboard. Shortly after the aircraft settled deeper in the water and, almost reluctantly, slipped beneath the waves.

The water lapped over the sides of the rubber dinghy causing cold and discomfort to the crew. It would also impede progress when the paddles were produced in the hope that further distance could be placed between themselves and the enemy. Pick, with the largest feet by far, removed his shoes and these were used to bale out the incoming water. From his battle dress tunic he removed the top button. This he unscrewed, with the bottom of the button parting from the RAF crested top. The base of the button contained a compass which had been given to him by his wife, Dorothy, at the beginning of war. He handed it to Alan Broadley.

'Right, Alan,' he said with resignation, 'it's over to you now! Remember the Ancient Mariner? You are now the instant mariner!'

Under Alan Broadley's direction, the crew took it in turns to keep the paddles working and head generally in the direction of the English coastline. It was a long, dark and difficult haul at first, but all six settled down to the paddling and baling routine, encouraged in the knowledge that a search would soon be mounted and their chances of being spotted and recovered were only a matter of time. . . .

Back at Newmarket Racecourse, Dorothy was asleep in the married quarters close to the airfield. Ming was resting by her bed, and for the greatest part of the night, was content. In the small and early hours, Dorothy was awakened by Ming as she tugged at the bed clothes. Resisting the interruption to her sleep in view of the hour, Dorothy turned over, quietly cursing all dogs, and Ming in particular. Ming would have none of it. Persistently, almost violently, Ming not so gently removed the blankets from the bed.

Under protest Dorothy arose, glanced at the clock which read twenty minutes past three, donned her gown, and opened the door for Ming to attend to the needs of nature. Outside in the garden, Ming made no effort to tend the needs of nature. She sat on her haunches, looked upwards at the sky, to left and to right, and continued her extraordinary action for some time. Dorothy left the door open, Ming in the garden, and made for the telephone. She rang the operations room at Newmarket.

'Any news?' asked Dorothy.

'Yes, Mrs Pickard' came the reply, 'six went out and five came back. "O for Orange" is missing.'

Without a word, Dorothy quietly replaced the telephone and sat on her bed. Ming had followed her into the house and sat looking at Dorothy. The thought of Ming looking up at the sky, to left and to right, while in the garden did little to reassure Dorothy.

Towards six o'clock in the morning, wrapped in a coat against adverse weather and with Ming following close behind, Dorothy walked out of the house and made for the end of the runway where she could already see aircraft taking off in quick succession. Beyond the runway and among the grass, Dorothy found an old tree stump on which she sat throughout the day. The aircraft continued to take off and land for refuelling. Every serviceable machine on the station was thrown into the search for Pick and the crew of 'O for Orange'. All morning, and for most of the afternoon, Ming sat on her haunches scanning the sky to left and to right. The weather was not unkind and late in the afternoon, Ming lay down to sleep.

At six o'clock in the evening, Dorothy telephoned the officer in charge of the ops room. He was none too gentle. He, too, was on edge.

'Where have you been?' he asked without ceremony.

'Out,' replied Dorothy, 'out all day.'

'Well,' continued the operations room expert, 'we found the dinghy this afternoon, but it was in the middle of a minefield and we had to allow it to drift out. All the crew are in the dinghy and we have been dropping supplies to them. Please bring a dry set of clothes for Pick. We expect to have them ashore between seven and eight o'clock.'

Dorothy replaced the receiver, packed what clothes she could and with some time on hand decided to wash Ming and tie a large red ribbon on Ming's head. This complete, she set off for the mess to be taken by transport to meet the cold, wet crew. Fourteen hours after ditching, Pick and the crew of 'O for Orange' were recovered from the sea by a fast launch from Air Sea Rescue. To compensate for their ordeal in the water, the entire crew were taken off flying duties for ten days.

The evening after their rescue, Pick and Dorothy were invited by the author, J B Priestley, for dinner and a show. The show, in which Vera Lynn starred, was packed to capacity mostly with service personnel. When Vera Lynn closed her act with the memorable and inevitable theme song 'We'll Meet Again', the words had a very special significance for Dorothy. As Vera sang, Dorothy remembered the ages which were two nights ago, being wakened by Ming and going out to the garden as the clock read twenty minutes past three in the cold morning. Amidst the standing ovation which greeted the end of Vera's song, Dorothy turned to Pick and asked if he could remember, exactly, when they had ditched.

'Very easy,' replied Pick, as he drew his broken watch from his pocket which he had meant to have repaired. 'My watch stopped when I was thrown against the instrument panel.'

He handed the watch to Dorothy. The glass was smashed and the hands were stationary. The time on the watch was 3.20.

CHAPTER FOUR

Target for To-night

Throughout June and July, still flying from Newmarket, the same crew continued their operations against Germany. Wilhelmshaven, Gotha, Bremen, Hamburg and the Ruhr received their attention regularly. By the end of July 1940, Pick and his crew had completed 31 operations in a three month stint, from Norway to Germany, the Low Countries and Italy. They were due for a rest.

Towards the end of July the crew was grounded and Pick was posted to command No 311 (Czech) Squadron at East Wretham in Norfolk. As he had found Alan Broadley indispensable in the air, he requested that Alan accompany him to the Czech squadron as the navigation officer. This request was granted and together they joined 311 Squadron on 29th July.

Charles Pickard was not impressed by being removed from operations but his experience in flying different types of aircraft ranged back to 1936, with very recent and extensive operations over enemy territory. With his kind and understanding disposition on the ground added to his fearless determination in the air, he was ideal to impart knowledge and inspire confidence. This he did with the same enthusiasm which was characteristic of all his flying.

The language difficulty made progress slow at first but this was resolved in a squadron of Czechs who were impatient to learn and had their sights set on active operations in the shortest possible time. Wellingtons and the slower, smaller, but equally sound Ansons were flown every day, with frequently as many as four instructional flights in one day. Dual, cross countries, flying tests and air firing were the order of the day. In August the Czechs under Pickard received their first bit of excitement and a taste of things to come. While on a dual cross country flight in an Anson, Pick spotted a Heinkel bomber which he knew he would be unable to intercept, and, even if he could, being unarmed he would be unable to attack.

On the RT he called ground control, asking for immediate fighter support. The fighters scrambled at once and Pick gave them a course to steer to vector on the Heinkel which he continued to shadow. The German crew of the Heinkel obviously recognised the Anson for what it was and treated it with the disdain the Anson did not deserve. With Fighter Command airfields and satellite aerodromes scattered below, Pick was soon joined by fighters raring to go. The disrespect with which the Heinkel had treated the Anson was to prove costly. The moment the Heinkel spotted the fighters, it turned tail and headed for the east coast. The fighters were content to allow the Heinkel to high-tail it to the coast and clear the countryside below before moving in. At maximum speed the Anson followed and was in time to see the Heinkel, mauled and destroyed by a jubilant pack of fighters, smoke its way down to the sea.

Pick found the Czechs to be a very brave and singularly superstitious people. Their superstitions became most marked before taking off for a raid. In odd pieces of garment which were never otherwise worn, they would be fully dressed and ready for briefing, looking an incongruous lot. They listened intently to their briefing instructions, following every word of the CO whom they had now come to respect and regard with affection, and had one ritual which they carried out religiously before taking off.

In the mess, the well known and well worn record 'So Deep Is the Night' was placed on the gramophone. The sounds of this moving piece of music filled the entire mess with never another word spoken. Each of the Czechs would move around the room, weaving in time to the music, transported by the music to another world. It became almost the national anthem of 311 Squadron. When the music ended, the Czechs were ready to move off, refreshed in mind and with dedication of purpose.

One day the irrepressible Sidney 'Timbertoes' Carlin whom Pick had not seen since the Kenya days telephoned Wittering and asked to speak to the commanding officer. He would not disclose his business and advised the exchange that it was entirely a personal matter, and the caller was an old personal friend. Sidney Carlin was put through.

'Pick?' began Sidney, 'Carlin here. Kenya Carlin. Timbertoes!'

'Where on earth are you and what are you doing?' asked Pick, unable to conceal his pleasure at hearing from his old, wild, horse-riding friend.

'Just down the road,' replied Sidney, 'just down the road, and I am doing nothing. That is why I am phoning. All I do is stooge around as the gunner on clapped out Defiants and I want to go on a raid in a Wellington!'

Pick knew very well that when Sidney Carlin made up his mind to do something, all the King's horses would be run off their feet trying to stop him. The irrepressible Sidney.

As the clouds of war were looming over Europe Sidney Carlin, at the age of 46, decided to return to England to fly as a pilot in the RAF. As a pilot, his application was turned down, but that did not deter Sidney who already wore the flying brevet of the RFC. As a marksman, his days in the open among the big game of East Africa had only served to increase his ability. He asked that he be allowed to be given any test, reminding the authorities that he had come all the way from Kenya to re-join the RAF and had done this not without difficulty. Travelling by dhow from Mombasa, the dhow had been sunk during a storm in the Red Sea, but Sidney had managed to swim ashore and make his way to Suez.

The tenacity of purpose to the point of bullying the authorities paid off and Sidney Carlin became a gunner in Defiant night fighters. He was one of two men entitled to wear the air gunner's badge and RFC pilot's brevet at that time.* He wore the two distinct badges on alternate uniforms! When he called his friend Pickard in February of 1941 he was Pilot Officer Carlin. Timbertoes' indomitable spirit was respected by Pick, and he knew, in any case, that there was no use arguing.

'Right,' answered Pick, 'I'll fix it!'

On the night of 18th February 1941, Pilot Officer Carlin flew in Wellington 1371 as rear gunner to his old friend Charles Pickard. They bombed Bremen, with Timbertoes sitting in the back enjoying the fireworks. His initiation over Germany only whetted his appetite for operations and he became a regular crew member with Pick, whenever he had seven days leave! It was a welcome change for Timbertoes who would sit for hours cramped up in a Defiant waiting for the 'scramble' order. With his wooden leg he did not want to hold

* The other was Flight Lieutenant Fielding-Johnson, MC DFC.

up his aircraft, or the pilot, in any way.

The successful operation over Bremen called for a celebration at which Sidney Carlin insisted on playing host.

'After all,' he told Pick, 'you delivered me out of the jaws of mine enemy!'

The party of six set out from Wittering and included Dorothy and Group Captain Baronski, the officer in charge of the Czechs. Driving the large estate car was Wing Commander Toman with Dorothy in the front for whom special dispensation had to be obtained as civilians were not allowed the use of RAF transport. Again, Pick managed to bend the rules.

They drove to an hotel which had been an old coaching house as a tribute to Timbertoes' life-long love of horses and had a very pleasant dinner party. At ten o'clock they decided to return to Wittering as they had taken off for Germany at midnight and had spent over five hours in the air.

Returning along the main road to Thetford, Dorothy in the front saw some lights ahead. The car did not appear to be slowing down. She glanced across at the driver, Wing Commander Toman, and noticed that he was sound asleep! In a flash, Dorothy reached over and swung the steering wheel to the right. The estate car was much too close and with a screech of grinding metal, they hit the obstacle ahead. It was a large pantechnicon furniture lorry.

Toman was instantly awake, applied the brakes automatically, but the car hit the ditch on the right hand side, throwing Sidney Carlin out. Everywhere was broken glass, rent metal, and blood. The driver of the pantechnicon must have felt the bump as he stopped, returned to the offending car behind him, took one look inside and screamed out, 'Oh, my God!' He pushed off quickly to find help.

Sidney Carlin was sitting, very dazed, at the side of the road shouting out, 'Get my horse! Get my horse!' and Dorothy was first to his aid to try and tell him that he was not in Kenya now, he was in England, and 'please keep quiet as there is an air raid going on at the moment!' Pick appeared, his heavy greatcoat cut to ribbons. Together they tried to get the message through to Timbertoes that they had been in a car crash.

'Crash? Crash?' asked Timbertoes, 'what bloody crash?' as he looked vaguely about. 'Oh. My leg. What about my leg?'

'What about your leg?' asked Dorothy.

'Is it all right?' asked Sidney.

Dorothy looked down at Sidney's leg. The hollowed out artificial leg had been smashed to pieces, revealing a series of compartments. Inside these compartments, Sidney had packed maps of Germany and France, a compass, emergency rations, files, hacksaw blades and cigarettes. It was a complete escaper's kit! Timbertoes had gone on the raid with Pick hoping for the best but prepared for the worst.

The damage in the dark appeared worse than it was and they were taken to the hospital in Thetford with the Czechs 'moaning and groaning much better'. Toman the driver had broken ribs. Timbertoes had smashed his wooden leg, and the others were badly cut by the flying glass.

When they had been patched up in hospital, Timbertoes turned to Pick and said, 'You know, Pick? I think it is a damned sight safer over Germany!' For Pilot Officer Sidney Carlin his words were to prove strangely prophetic.

On 12th May 1941, Sidney Carlin had become a Flying Officer. For once he was not seated in his aircraft when a low level, sneak attack was made on his airfield. There had been no previous warning of an approaching raid. Sidney Carlin wasted no time in making for his aircraft, running as best he could across the tarmac, waving at the oncoming enemy machine and calling out, 'You bastard! You bloody bastard!'

Timbertoes Carlin was gunned down as he ran. He was 48 years old.

The task of RAF Wittering where Pick was in charge of the training and working up the squadron to operational readiness, while Alan Broadley was in charge of navigation, was not without its lighter moments.

There was a shortage of pilots for the Wellingtons and Pick decided to call for qualified pilots with the maximum number of hours in the first instance to carry out a conversion course to the Wellington. On his arrival, and through an interpreter, he called for volunteers who were keen to convert, into the crew room. He explained the position as slowly and clearly as he could, allowing time for the interpreter to translate.

'Our need is for more pilots to fly our Wellingtons. We have to be ready to attack targets over Germany in the shortest possible time. I would like your full co-operation. To set the ball rolling, it will make life easier and complete the conversion more quickly if I have those with the greatest number of flying hours.'

This was duly translated and a murmur spread around the assembled flying personnel. There was an immediate rush of applications to be first to convert and each recorded his number of flying hours, as closely as they could remember, few if any, being in possession of their own flying log books. Of these, a certain Flight Lieutenant Joe Snajdr approached the table and advised the interpreter that he had 2,000 flying hours which represented a considerable amount of flying in 1940. Pick was more than impressed and decided to make Joe Snajdr his first star pupil as an indication to the others of how it is done and how to do it in the shortest possible time.

Joe was detailed to make ready for his first dual instruction flight in the Wellington. Pick sat on his left in the first pilot's seat and ran through the full and comprehensive instrument panel and the vital action drill before take-off. Allowance had to be made for the language problem and patience was of the essence. The Czechs had a twofold problem – learning the names of the various instruments and their functions, at the same time putting everything together in the unusually large, if docile, Wellington, ready for take-off. It was a unique experience for Pick, trying to teach a man to fly with words of instruction which conveyed nothing! He decided to take the aircraft off the ground without further ado and point to the instruments most needed for the take-off performance. He was convinced that, once in the air, he would be able to hand over the aircraft to his pupil to allow him to become acquainted with the controls. Straight and level. Climbing, turns, and the sluggishness of the aircraft at the point of stall. A man with 2,000 flying hours should be able to fly by the seat of his pants in any language and in almost any aircraft in a matter of two or three hours.

Pick's reasoning received a rude shock on the first flight with Joe. His 'star' pupil seemed to have the utmost difficulty in flying straight and level. Turns became out of the question as the aircraft slewed round with Joe holding off bank for all he was worth and it was a worried CO who brought the Wellington in to land. Pick was not impressed with the potential of Czech pilots with 2,000 flying hours. Still, a strange language, a strange aircraft and different conditions on the ground and in the air could contribute towards a ham-fisted performance and Pick was prepared to give Joe the benefit of the doubt.

Twenty flying hours later, Pick decided that he could stand it no longer and blew his top. He called for the interpreter. In words which rarely ran to more than four letters, Pick gave Joe the tongue lashing of his life. Pick made an exception to his use of four letter words by screaming at his pupil, 'Ullage!' 'Ullage!' which, being freely translated means, 'Useless!' 'Rubbish!'

Joe stood with eyes unblinking in front of the massive and dreaded CO.

'How can any man, short of an idiot,' shouted Pick, 'tell me that he has 2,000 flying hours as a pilot and fly like a drunken sailor after 20 hours on the simplest of aircraft? You are ullage, real absolute ullage!'

Pick's pride and his faith in his fellow man reached an all time low. After the tirade, Joe added insult to injury. He smiled.

'Me not pilot, Sir. Me observer, 2,000 hours observer!'

In a blazing temper which was fanned by the fumes of the petrol used by the Wellington in 20 hours' flying time, Pick decided that, come hell or high water, he would turn Joe Snajdr into a pilot. Joe became a pilot.

As the squadron became operationally efficient, it was Pick's habit always to make the first flight over enemy territory with his new pilots, to give them confidence and encouragement. He would take no active part in the flying of the machine but he would just be on hand in case anything went wrong or the pilot needed advice. He would settle down comfortably somewhere in the middle of the aircraft, well wrapped up against the altitude and the cold.

Sooner or later it was Joe Snajdr's turn to make his first fully fledged operation over Germany. The target was Berlin, and Pick settled down in his back seat to await the outcome of his 'star' pupil on a raid. The aircraft took-off without hitting anything, climbed on course and made for the English Channel. So far, so good, thought Pick. The aircraft levelled off high over the channel with the engines throbbing sweetly and Pick began to think of a bit of shut-eye. Suddenly the regular tenor of the engines was broken by the voice of Joe shouting over the RT. 'Landing! Landing!'

Pick roused himself from his quiet and warm thoughts and made his way to the cockpit. He opened the door to the cockpit and was met by a freezing blast. Joe had omitted to check that the side window had been locked shut for take-off, the window had blown back and disappeared into the dark depths below.

'Landing, landing!' he shouted at Pick and pointed to the open gap in the perspex and to the ground.

With a hearty slap on the back from Charles Pickard, Joe Snajdr received news from his CO.

'Berlin! Berlin!' screamed back Pick and he flung his arm straight ahead. Joe knew better than to argue with Pick while in the air. He flew to Berlin.

By the time they had returned to base Joe Snajdr was a solid block of ice from the neck up and had to be carried from the aircraft. Before Joe was sent down to Torquay for a month to recover from frostbite he received a word of advice from his mentor.

'Let that be a lesson to you, Joe,' began Pick. 'I am not worried about you. I am concerned with the safety of the crew and my precious aircraft. Next time, don't forget to close and lock all doors or hatches. You can read about it. It's in the book!'

Joe went off on leave to thaw out, a colder but a wiser man. The lesson was not lost on Joe. As intended by Pick, he had to learn the hard way and he did. He returned and went on to win a DFC. His association with Charles Pickard was not at an end. Joe married Dorothy's sister, Hilary, and the man with the frozen head became his brother-in-law.

It was with the Czech Squadron, that Charles Pickard first came to the notice of the British public. 1940 had been a grim year for Britain. Completely outnumbered in aircraft and airmen by the Germans who had transgressed the Versailles Peace Treaty which forbade the manufacture of military aircraft, Britain was in no condition to strike back. Raids on British soil were kept up with reckless abandon, and it seemed to the British public that nothing, or very little, was being done in retaliation. It was the blackest year of the war.

The British Government were conscious of the feelings of the general public and plans were made in the winter of 1940 to produce a film as close to a documentary as possible, of raids being carried out against targets in Germany. The film would show the crews, briefing and preparation, take-off into the night sky, flying over the enemy target, bombs away, and returning from the raid, crippled. The title of the film would be *Target for To-night* and the 'star' chosen to lead the raid would be Charles Pickard in a Wellington bomber, known as 'F for Freddie'.

It was from the release of this dramatic film that Charles Pickard became known to millions of Britons as 'F for Freddie', a name with which he was to be affectionately remembered and with which his future exploits would be associated. In the film, the pipe-smoking Pickard was easily recognisable by his towering height, his blond hair, and his nonchalant manner in the part of Squadron Leader Dixon. It was a classic of the time.

The British public were in sore need of seeing some action, headed by their popular idea of a hero. In the giant, blond Yorkshireman they were not disappointed. That Pick was an inveterate pipe smoker by nature only enhanced the image of quiet thinking, and resolute strength. His own reaction when he was first asked to star in a film to boost morale was one of disbelief, consternation, and a string of expletives. He removed his pipe for the expletives.

The film was made at Blackheath Studios and was directed by Harry Watt. It meant taking time off from 311 Squadron in March of 1941, and for a couple of weeks in April. With the minimum of props, less of known stars and a natural desire from the cast just to be themselves, it became an enormous success.

Unknown to the people of Britain, behind the making of the film, both Dorothy and Pick were to experience their own personal and terrible drama. Through Pick's sister, Helena, Dorothy and Pick were offered a flat in London. The block of flats was owned by Harold Kahn, a very wealthy gentleman who had spent his earlier years in South Africa. The block of flats stood at the corner of Jermyn Street and Duke Street in London, and the flat was put at the disposal of Dorothy and Pick for as long as it was required.

Whenever shooting was necessary for the film, Pick would be advised in advance and this would give them time to travel from Wittering to London, and they would make straight for the flat in Jermyn Street. Half way through the making of the film, they received a request to be ready for an appearance in four days' time. Together they made the journey to London, en route for the flat. An air raid had taken place the previous night and a great deal of debris littered the streets as they approached the flats. Apart from a litter of glass on the ground in front of the flats, everything appeared to be intact. They entered the foyer of the flats and met an absolute shambles.

The block had received a direct hit the night before. Only the outer shell of the building remained, apparently intact, while the inside was a maze of rubble. Bodies lay on the floor of the foyer, wrapped in canvas bags, with the dust still blowing down from the shattered inside walls. Among those in the canvas coffins was their friend, Al Bowley, the well known London singer who had occupied the flat next to the Pickards. The destruction was the work of a land mine, and nothing of value remained.

The mute testimony to indiscriminate bombing, created by the sight of the canvas bags in the foyer, made a deep and lasting impression on Charles Pickard. He was never to forget. After his return to Wittering on completion of the film, 'F for Freddie' was transferred to command No 9 Squadron, and his first operation with his new squadron satisfied the frustrated anger he had felt at Jermyn Street in London.

On 27th May he went to sea in a Wellington, searching for the *Prinz Eugen* . . .

The order to search for the *Prinz Eugen* which was carried out by Charles Pickard in a Wellington from No 9 Squadron began a series of events in which the Royal Air Force and the Royal Navy became increasingly involved.

Pick led the first operational sweep from No 9 Squadron to help avenge the sinking of the *Hood* by the *Bismarck*. The stunned silence which followed the sinking, left a deep feeling of the need for revenge among the British public. Charles Pickard felt that he was in a

Target for tonight

position to translate his feelings into action. The war had to be won, whatever the cost. Eight hours and twenty-five minutes later the squadron returned without sighting *Prinz Eugen*. The exercise began as an order and finished as a fiasco.

This briefly is the background to the operation. It had been Admiral Raeder's plan to send the concentrated force of the *Scharnhorst, Gneisenau, Bismarck,* and *Prinz Eugen* into the Atlantic in May of 1941, backed up by an increased U-boat campaign, to paralyse British shipping. In the last seven months of 1940 over three million tons of British, Allied and neutral ships had been sent to the bottom. The *Scharnhorst* and the *Gneisenau*, in a seven week cruise in the North Atlantic, had sunk or captured 22 ships totalling 116 600 tons. The total sinkings were 400 000 tons in February and over half a million tons in March.

Damage suffered by the *Scharnhorst* on her last cruise could not be repaired in time for the rendezvous in May and in April the *Gneisenau* was spotted by a PRU Spitfire and photographed in the harbour at Brest. This was one of the war's most decisive photographs. When the presence of the ships at Brest became known, they became a primary objective of Bomber Command.

The task was given to 22 Squadron commanded by Group Captain F J St G Braithwaite. In the attack, Flying Officer Kenneth Campbell received a posthumous VC for his gallant attack which resulted in severely damaging *Gneisenau*.

The *Bismarck* and the *Prinz Eugen* lay await in Norway for thick and suitable weather before breaking out and making for the Atlantic. The Admiralty was particularly concerned about the *Bismarck*. All available resources of the Royal Navy were required to track her down and sink her.

The lengthening days of May 1941 added a new dimension of danger and watchfulness to the aircraft of Coastal Command and to the Spitfires attached to the Photographic Reconnaissance Unit (PRU) of the Royal Air Force. The lifelines of Britain were in jeopardy by the action of the U-Boat packs in the Atlantic and there was the ever present danger of the capital ships moving out to attack the North Atlantic convoys.

From St Eval in Cornwall, the Northern French coastline could be watched and photographed by Spitfires. Wick in the North of

Scotland, with the Spitfires operating out of a remote airfield on the bare cliffs of Caithness allowed flights to be made which spanned the Norwegian coast. The pilots remained alert to spot any German ships slipping out towards the open sea.

It was from Wick on 21st May 1941, that the work being conducted by PRU came into its own.

On the Wednesday morning news came through from the Admiralty marked 'most urgent' to say that information had been received of 'German ships' steaming north in the Kattegat on the 20th. There was no indication of the nature of the 'ships', nor was a hint dropped as to what they might be, but the course and speed indicated that by the 21st they must be somewhere off the Norwegian coastline. This being so, it was the duty of the PRU Spitfires to find them and photograph them. They would be within range.

Two Spitfires were made ready and two pilots were standing by to fly them. Of the two, Flying Officer Greenhill was an experienced DFC while the other, Pilot Officer Michael Suckling, was his junior, but not lacking in operational experience.

Suckling arrived back at Wick at 02.30 hours. His excitement could hardly be contained.

'I've seen them! Two of them! I think they are cruisers although one could be a battleship!' he shouted to the two members of his PRU interpreting staff who met him at the end of the runway. The waiting airmen quickly removed the magazines from the cameras and rushed back to the photographic section.

It was indeed a battleship. *The* battleship.

Warning of the northward movement was reported to London and intensive patrolling and search by Coastal Command aircraft was at once started. Later the same day the enemy ships were discovered in Korsfiord, a short distance south of Bergen. They were being re-fuelled before sailing north the same evening.

Admiral Sir John Tovey, as Commander-in-Chief of the British Home Fleet, was anxiously awaiting news of their movements and he immediately took steps to intercept. The Admiralty placed at his disposal all the heavy ships that could be spared.

On board the battle cruiser *Hood*, Admiral Holland calculated a course to intercept and prepared for action at any time after 01.40 on 24th May. Contact was not made until 05.35 at which time the

Hood and the new battleship *Prince of Wales* advanced into action. Admiral Holland ordered a head-on approach, denying the use of the after guns. The Germans opened fire and concentrated on the *Hood*. Holland ordered a 20 degree turn to port, but scarcely had the ships begun to respond when the *Hood* was hit in the magazine by a shell from the *Bismarck* and disintegrated.

The news that the *Hood* had gone almost in an inkling was received at the Admiralty and in Britain with a stunned silence. The pride of the Royal Navy and backbone of Britain's sea defences was no more. The stunned silence was not allowed to last and efforts were redoubled to bring the *Bismarck* to book.

The British forces continued to shadow the two German ships throughout the day. Suddenly the *Bismarck* turned on the cruiser *Suffolk* which opened range and beat a hasty retreat. This move was made to cover the departure of the *Prinz Eugen* which escaped to the south.

During the night, all forces raced to the probable position of the *Bismarck*. By the morning of 26th May the pursuers began to lose hope. Now well out in the Atlantic, the British ships were subject to possible U-Boat attacks and were forced to take zig-zag courses to cover this contingency. For a time all contact was lost with the *Bismarck*.

Suddenly, at 10.30 on the morning of the 26th a Catalina of Coastal Command spotted a battleship approximately 750 miles west of Brest. This information was relayed to the Royal Navy and a quick plotting check was made. It was no British battleship. The *Bismarck* had been found.

Throughout the night British destroyers shadowed the *Bismarck* and by morning the battleships *Rodney* and *King George V* reached the scene of action. The *Bismarck*, although badly crippled, through a torpedo dropped by Lieutenant Commander Eugene Esmonde of the Fleet Air Arm still had magnificent endurance and excellent fire control. The weight of British fire power began to tell and the *Bismarck* was hit in her main battery director early in the action which diminished the accuracy of her fire appreciably. But she refused to sink. Admiral Tovey, with barely enough fuel to get home, had to break off. The cruiser *Dorsetshire* requested permission to expend her last three torpedoes on the *Bismarck* before leaving. As her third torpedo struck home the *Bismarck* rolled slowly over and disappeared beneath the waves. The *Hood* was avenged.

Back in Britain, concern was expressed for the whereabouts of the *Prinz Eugen*. On 27th May, Charles Pickard was ordered out as formation leader to search for the *Prinz Eugen* in Wellingtons. The *Prinz Eugen* steered south to avoid the attention of the Royal Navy in its massive hunt for the *Bismarck* before making for Brest at the beginning of June. On 7th June, Winston Churchill's words were again carried out to the letter and in Wellington T 5703, Pickard started Bomber Command's pursuit of shipping in Biscayan ports Their target was the much harried *Prinz Eugen* but she was not to be found. The *Scharnhorst*, *Gneisenau* and *Prinz Eugen* suffered repeated air attacks from the Royal Air Force in Brest and had to keep their heads down until February of 1942 when they made a break up the English Channel to reach the waters off the Dutch coast in the famous and humiliating Channel Dash.

CHAPTER FIVE

Bruneval

The tour of operational duty with No 9 Squadron which had begun with the search for the *Prinz Eugen* as formation leader was an indication to Charles Pickard and Alan Broadley that they had been thrown in on their second tour at the deep end.

Although the attention of the Royal Navy and the Royal Air Force had been heavily directed against the *Scharnhorst, Gneisenau* and the *Prinz Eugen* in Brest harbour after the sinking of the *Bismarck*, and prior to the final 'Channel Dash' on the implicit instructions of Winston Churchill, targets in Europe could not be neglected. Two days after bombing the *Prinz Eugen*, No 9 Squadron was sent out against a target at Flushing in the Netherlands. Heavy anti-aircraft fire and fighters over the target accounted for two of No 9 Squadron's Wellingtons and the loss of two aircraft and their crews was a sad blow to the operational efficiency of the squadron. Britain was suffering from a shortage of both.

During the month of June, Dusseldorf received regular attention from the squadron and by the end of the month, Charles Pickard and Alan Broadley had completed a total of 55 operational sorties together.

July and August followed in like fashion with the targets looking like a 'Who's Who' of German industry. Essen, Cologne, Munster, Bremen, Hamburg, Hanover and Mannheim. The strain of two completed tours of operations by August of 1941 and a total of 65 flights at night over heavily defended targets, with regular practice flights in between, is a fair quota for most men. There were several ways of easing the strain and relaxing the tension, but to Pick the panacea to all ills lay on the back of a horse or the cockpit of a Tiger Moth. On horseback he rode out regularly with Dorothy and Ming on rabbit excursions in the early mornings after a raid, returning with a ravenous appetite for breakfast. This completed, he would ask for the station Tiger Moth to be made ready for 'solo aerobatics'. Both offered an agreeable change from the monotony of straight and level flying when flak and fighters were the only unwelcome diversion.

On 10th August a rest period was indicated and both airmen were posted to 3 Group. For Pick, his rest period consisted mainly of ferrying VIP's around the country in Miles Mentors and Whitleys. One of these was Air Marshal Sir John Baldwin whose son, Tony, was one of Pick's closest friends. Tony Baldwin did not follow in his father's footsteps into the Air Force but elected to join the 8th Hussars instead. Very sadly, Tony Baldwin was killed in action in the Western Desert in Rommel's final and last success.

Although technically on a rest from operations, before the month was out Pick wheedled his way back on two operations, one in a Whitley to Chatreau in France and the second in a Wellington to Holland. The flight to Holland must constitute one of the oddest cargoes of the war at that time. Holland was in the grip of the German occupying forces and there was a severe shortage of cigarettes. It was the duty of Charles Pickard and his crew to deliver 500,000 cigarettes to the smoke addicts of Holland. For good measure, and to make the trip really worth while, the odd cargo was accompanied in the bomb bay by six 250 lb bombs. As an inveterate pipe smoker, Pick had no time for cigarettes.

'Cigarettes and bombs', he observed as the nature of his cargo became known, 'that's the quickest way to smoke yourself to death!'

Three months with 3 Group passed in continuous flying, ferrying and instruction in an assortment of light aircraft. Leave was long overdue and with the coming of winter restricting flying activities, Pick pushed off for the month of November. On his return, at the same time as Alan Broadley, once more they were posted together, to 51 Squadron. They were back on Whitleys and celebrated the festive season by visiting Boulogne, Emden, St Nazaire, Fecamp and Etretat. On these trips they were less aggressive, perhaps with deference to the spirit of the season. Not a single bomb was dropped, but many photographs were taken . . .

Germany had evolved a system of radar detection which indicated the approach of British aircraft to the French or Low Countries coastline at ranges of 200 to 250 miles. On occasion their radar could pick up British aircraft being marshalled into one force over the British Isles. As night bomber attacks from Britain developed, it became increasingly necessary to take direct action against this system to prevent it from inflicting serious losses on the bomber formations. The enemy had to be stopped from having ample time to make night-fighter dispositions to attack the incoming bombers.

Photographic reconnaissance was not a new technique to be started in 1939. No 70 Squadron of the Royal Flying Corps with other units pioneered the idea with varying degrees of success and some disastrous failures. In the course of three days, No 70 Squadron, RFC, had lost all three Flight Commanders and all its most experienced crews while attempting to carry out photographic reconnaissance. In their final sortie of six aircraft not a single machine returned. Lack of speed in the earlier aircraft caused a grievous loss of life among those engaged in aerial photography. By 1939, this message had been received and understood.

To take photographs from a fast flying aircraft was one thing. To have them intelligently and fully interpreted was another. By trial and error, with some brilliant boffins in the back room and enthusiastic pilots in the air, the Photographic Reconnaissance Unit of the RAF made remarkable strides.

Flight Lieutenant Tony Hill was of that rare breed who are able to combine efficiency with enthusiasm. He specialised in taking oblique photographs of radar installations from a low height. Almost by accident Tony Hill had called at Medmenham where PRU work was being developed from his station at Benson which was about fifteen miles away. He was invited into the holy of holies to have a look at a couple of photographs. The photographs showed a portion of French coastline with an isolated house near the edge of high cliffs.

"Where exactly is this place?" asked Tony Hill.

'It's Cap d'Antifer, near le Havre', he was told with the laughing rejoinder, 'you pilots annoy me. You go in over this place time and time again and never turn on your cameras soon enough!'

With the hallmark of a decisive and confident man of action, Tony Hill replied, 'I'll get you the answer tomorrow.'

The following day, Tony Hill was booked out for Etretat, close by the small village of Bruneval. The camera in his aircraft failed to work and this made another sortie necessary. Against the rules of never flying the same sortie two days in succession, as the secret of success was the element of surprise, Tony Hill returned to Bruneval the next day. His close-ups were taken from so low that it was possible to see into the ground floor windows of the steep-roofed house near the radar installation. The interest of Tony Hill when he had been shown the two photographs at Medmenham and his impatient desire to get things done, combined to launch one of the earliest full combined operation of the war.

On 13th February 1942, Charles Pickard was to add grist to the Bruneval mill. He made a high level reconnaissance of Fécamp, Etretat and Bruneval in his Whitley. The nature of the terrain from his photographs, when analysed and assessed by photographic intelligence, would help the airborne forces considerably when they were dropped in strange and enemy territory.

Really good photographs are an excellent form of intelligence but the detailed planning that was necessary could not be done from photographs alone. It was at this point that Medmenham's most secret department – the Model Making Section – had to step in. It was far from a merely mechanical task. The photographs had to be translated into a different language – into three dimensional replicas instead of a normal written report.

At the time the Bruneval raid was being planned, the cellars at Danesfield were the setting for this highly secret activity. Flight Lieutenant Geoffrey Deeley, a sculptor in peacetime, worked with a staff of specialists, many of whom were also sculptors or artists. Any photographs which they could obtain of the area were translated by fret-saw, spatula and paint-brush into a precise miniature related to heights, distances and features surrounding the Bruneval district. No pains were spared and no detail overlooked into the planning of converting the Bruneval radio-location post into a radio-dislocation post. The cliffs at Cap d'Antifer were given their height. The little valley near Bruneval its gentle slope. Buildings, trees and fences were all placed in their relative positions, and to scale. In the end, by bending down and looking along the surface of the model, it was possible to see exactly what the airborne forces were going to encounter. This was the model which the troops and the aircrews were to study with infinite care, inspired by self preservation, before the raid on the night of 27th February 1942.

The radio-location post itself could have been wiped out at a stroke by the aircraft of Bomber Command. In so doing, the secrets of the German radio-location post would have been lost and Britain was anxious to ascertain the extent and the improvements to the enemy's radar equipment. The exercise demanded the services of experts in their various fields. The Royal Air Force to fly the airborne troops safely and accurately to Bruneval. The airborne troops with every man knowing precisely his job. The regular army to help in any rearguard action to facilitate the recovery of the airborne troops and the Royal Navy to recover both from the beaches. Added to the airborne troops for the occasion, the Royal Air Force lent Flight Sergeant C. W. H. Cox, who was an expert in radar, and it would be the job of Flight Sergeant Cox to dismantle the apparatus, take photographs of anything which could not quickly be dismantled, and decide when the remainder should be consigned to high explosive charges set by the airborne troops.

The airborne forces were to be led by Major J. D. Frost of the Cameronians. Every inch of over six feet a soldier, Major Frost had followed in his father's footsteps to Sandhurst, fought in Palestine, and wore a ribbon of the Palestine Medal. When told that his troops would be flown by Whitleys of the Royal Air Force, led by Wing Commander P. C. Pickard, Major Frost was delighted and this added to his confidence and that of his men. Charles Pickard was known to them all as the pilot of the Wellington bomber in the film *Target for To-night* and thereafter his distinguished career had been followed with almost a personal interest. The ships which were to take the airborne troops back to England were under the command of Commander F Norton Cook of the Royal Australian Navy. The assault landing craft and support landing craft were under the command of Lieutenant Commander W G Everett of the Royal Navy.

Later Major Frost was to report . . .

'We were all concentrated down on Salisbury Plain to practise. Pickard's squadron had been taken off bombing operations and sent to Abingdon in the old fashioned Whitley bombers, very slow but very safe. I went over there one day with my officers to meet the aircrews and particularly the pilots. When we arrived, the Wing Commander wasn't there. I don't quite know where he was, but, having had a good look round we were having tea in the mess when suddenly he came in – a tremendously bustling, powerful figure, and the first thing he said to his pilots was, 'Why the Hell aren't you in the air flying?'

'His pilots replied that they were telling their opposite numbers in the airborne forces about their problems. Anyhow, he soon joined in the party and we knew, having now met him and them, that they were going to do an absolutely first class job for us.

'The next time I met him was when we did the first practice drop from his aircraft and once again we were greatly impressed by the efficiency of the squadron. They arrived to pick us up at Netheravon airfield bang on time and everything went like clockwork, and I must say that this was, again, a great fillip to our morale.

'We met again at Thruxton airfield just before we emplaned to be taken over for the operation. Once again we were more than impressed by the way the aircraft were positioned and with the way everything seemed to function absolutely as it should. The only thing that slightly worried me was what old Pick said to me just before take-off.

'He said "I feel like a bloody murderer, dropping you poor devils over there in a foreign country when we are all nice and peaceful here!"

'However, I thought no more about it because this was the job we had to do. In the event, the aircraft had to fly straight across the channel and rendezvous over le Havre. Le Havre was defended fairly strongly with anti-aircraft guns and some of the aircraft were hit while we were circling. Then we turned north and made for our dropping zone.'

Major Frost had divided his forces into three parties of unequal numbers. The task of Frost and 'C' Company was to give cover to Flight Sergeant Cox and a section of the 1st Parachute Field Squadron of the Royal Engineers under Captain Dennis Vernon, while the radar station was being dismantled, photographed and the highly valuable parts removed to the waiting ships which were due off-shore on completion of the operation.

Ranged against them, the Germans had signallers and covering troops on duty at the radar post and the nearby villa which accounted for approximately thirty men. A further hundred were in immediate support and were stationed in a cluster of farm buildings known as La Presbytere about three hundred yards to the north of the villa. Finally the village of Bruneval itself. Here the garrison numbered forty and their job was to man the pillboxes and earthworks guarding the village and the beach. The evacuation had to be made from the beach and the fortified pillboxes were located both on top of the cliffs and on the beach itself. Major Frost was reminded of Pick's favourite expression, 'There is always a bloody something!' Still, Frost could only hope that the Navy would be on time bringing the infantry to help in the rearguard action and to get his airborne troops off the beach with the minimum number of casualties.

Code-named 'Drake', 'Nelson' and 'Rodney', the largest to which Flight Sergeant Cox and Captain Vernon were attached was 'Drake' and consisted of fifty men. These were subdivided into two groups with Lieutenant Peter Young, an ex-Fleet Street man, to take care of the radar post itself and Major Frost to attack the villa. Lieutenant E. C. B. Charteris of the King's Own Scottish Borderers would lead the party known as Nelson with forty men in close support, and the detachment Rodney was due to arrive last. Lieutenant John Timothy of the Royal West Kent Regiment had thirty men in Rodney and their job was to deal with any Germans advancing to counter attack either at the radar post or on the beach.

An *estaminet* is a French drinking house and it was known that Bruneva possessed one which was 'fairly well appointed'. On the night of 27th February the airborne troops hoped that it would be well patronised. It was decided that Major Frost should give the signal to attack by blowing a whistle just as he approached the door of the villa.

'And if the door is locked?' he was asked.

'Ring the bell!' suggested one of his men.

From 24th February until the 27th the 119 men involved suffered frustrating postponements. The weather had to be exactly right with fairly good visibility and the tide suitable for the Navy. A full moon and a high tide generally go hand in hand. Fog or a heavy ground mist for such an operation could nullify both. On the afternoon of the 27th, in place of the staff officer, Major General Browning himself arrived to say that they were to take off that night. The weather was at last favourable. 'No wind, a bright moon, a little cloud and a light haze.'

The troops were jubilant, and marched round the perimeter of Thruxton like guardsmen behind pipers playing the regimental marches of Scotland. A mug of tea well laced with rum 'just in case it was cold' and the twelve sticks entered the twelve Whitleys. At the last moment Major Frost was called to the telephone. It was Group Captain Sir Nigel Norman, the Force Commander. 'France', he told Frost, 'is covered in snow and the light anti-aircraft defences seem to be particularly alert.'

The die was cast. The Whitleys lined the tarmac and the airborne forces emplaned.

From time to time Pick fed back news of the aircraft's progress and position. Between the tea, rum, sleeping bags and the singing of 'Come Sit by My Side If You Love Me' the troops tried to keep warm. The song they sang is the special song of the Parachute Regiment and only the first line is printable. In words to songs, the barrack room and the ballroom are worlds apart.

Others played cards among whom was Corporal Stewart who was an inveterate card player and gambler. He carried a well filled wallet crammed with his ill gotten gains. In the relatively short time between England and France, Corporal Stewart was able to add to his bulging pouch. He may have been a gambler but he was also a fatalist.

'If I am hit,' he told his mates, 'the man nearest me is in luck and can help himself.'

Later, Corporal Stewart was hit by a splinter on the head which laid him low. Conscious of his meeting with his Maker and mindful of his winnings he called out to his nearest comrade, Lance Corporal Freeman.

'I've had it. Here's my wallet. Help yersel'.'

Carefully bending over his comrade, accepting the wallet and offering his most sincere felicitations, Lance Corporal Freeman examined the wound, clearing it with his emergency field dressing.

The Harrow Bomber in flight, 1937.

214 Squadron (HP Harrow Bombers). Pickard is ninth from the left.

Pickard's Harrow Bomber, K6993.

Dorothy and Charles Pickard, June 1940, the day after Pickard and his crew had endured 14 hours in their dinghy in the North Sea.

Pickard at peace with his pipe and two horses.

No 311 Squadron.

Czech and RAF officers of No 311 Squadron, and *(below)* the Squadron's English sheep dog mascot. Pickard is holding his pipe.

Reconnaissance photograph of the German radio location station at Bruneval.

An aerial plan of the Combined Operations raid on Bruneval.

With Stewart convinced that he was approaching the Pearly Gates fast, Freeman was able to re-assure him at once.

'You've only got a scalp wound,' Freeman advised.

'All right,' replied Corporal Stewart, 'gie us ma bluidy wallet back then.'

Corporal Stewart lived to dice another day.

The drop was not without incident. The last of the twelve Whitleys to approach the area at 00.25 hours in bright moonlight with its crew of Sergeants Cook, Storey, Cox, Craven and Flying Officer Booker had this to report:

> Aircraft dropped paratroops at Bruneval at 00.25 and 00.30 hours in the centre of the dropping zone. Two drops were necessary as No 6 hung up on the first run, he was hauled back into the aircraft and he and the remainder jumped on the second run. The parachutes were seen to open by the rear gunner and opened parachutes were seen discarded in the dropping zone. Four flak ships were sighted on the run-in, just off Fecamp, steaming south. They opened fire on the aircraft. A light gun on the coast also opened fire on the aircraft. Visibility was good – three to four miles. The aircraft returned safely to base.

Lieutenant Charteris and the 'Nelson' party had been dropped slightly at the wrong place. On the approach to the dropping area, some of the Whitleys had to alter course to avoid anti-aircraft fire. As a consequence they were late in arriving at the assembly point. Without the 'Nelson' party, Lieutenant Timothy and the 'Rodney' detachment were in dire straits and far from strong enough to attack the German pillboxes and the critical beach. When Charteris had landed with his group he realised at once that he was in the wrong place and at the wrong time. He was later to accede that this was a nasty moment. The valley looked like a valley, if not deep enough, but there was an agonising absence of trees where they should have been. The aircraft which Lieutenant Charteris had just left with his stick of nine men could be seen making a turn around to fly on a reciprocal course for base. This gave them a lead and they set off at a jog-trot in the direction of the aircraft's turn. Presently they caught sight of the Cap d'Antifer lighthouse and this gave them a true bearing on their position. They continued at a jog-trot.

Shortly, they made contact with the enemy in the form of a line of Germans moving in single file in the opposite direction. Slight confusion followed and the stick of ten men which had been dropped from the Whitley increased to eleven. One of the German troops had erred in the confusion and was happy to follow Lieutenant Charteris and his stick. His degree of happiness was short lived. When the error of his ways was discovered, it was a short step to Eternity. Charteris and his men soon rejoined Major Frost.

With the radar equipment dismantled and the remainder photographed, Lieutenant Charteris and his men were sent ahead to clear the beach by Major Frost. Stiff opposition was at first encountered from the pillboxes guarding the beach. Captain Vernon and Flight Sergeant Cox, accompanied by the sappers, were already in position with their invaluable equipment awaiting the arrival of the Royal Navy off-shore. It was the job of Lieutenant Charteris and his men to clear the reluctant pillboxes. The garrison of a nearby pillbox was speedily despatched, but there was still no sign of the Navy and the relieving forces to help with the beach encounter. From one of the pillboxes guarding the beach, a voice in impeccable English called out.

'The Navy's here! The Navy's here!'

This attempt at subterfuge by the Germans to entice the troops to the open ground on the beach was not misunderstood. One of the Seaforths crawled to the pillbox under covering fire, paused for a moment as he pulled out the pin of his hand grenade, and, calling out in his own impeccable English, 'get out, ye lyin' bastards', lobbed the grenade into the pillbox. The strict confines of a pillbox in the dark have few answers to a well placed hand grenade.

Surprise had been no little factor in the success of the operation. With faces blackened even to their teeth the troops, dropped from only a few hundred feet, had covered half a mile and were nearly at their objective before a shot was fired at them. It was only after the essential part of the operation was completed and the troops were making for the beach where the Navy were to embark them that they came up against serious opposition.

A charge by the Seaforth Highlanders, led by a sergeant, proved the turning point. The party attacking the beach had been pinned down for some time by accurate machine-gun fire from the beach fort. The minimum time for the raid had already expired and danger to the paratroops themselves grew as each minute passed. This danger equally increased for the light naval craft standing by to retrieve the men. Suddenly, above the noise of firing, the battle cry of the Seaforths could be heard.

'Cabar feidh!'

This indicated that one party of the paratroops had joined up with the main force and was now coming into action. ('Cabar feidh' is one of the Seaforth Highlanders' mottos and is Gaelic for 'Antlers of the Deer'.)

'Inside ten minutes,' reported Captain John Ross, the second in command, 'the beach was in our hands.'

The Germans holding the fort had all either been killed, captured or had fled to a nearby wood. Captain Ross, who emphasised what a complete surprise the raid was to the Germans, said he was sure that right up to the end the Germans did not know what was happening. Though they fought well so long as they held the attackers off, 'when it came to fighting at close quarters, they gave in'. They were stubborn when behind cover and in a good position, but if suddenly confronted at only a few yards – and much of the fighting was done at no greater range – they generally turned and ran.

One of the defenders ran to the edge of a cliff and dropped to a ledge below. He was pursued by twenty-two year old Lieutenant Young. Confronted by Lieutenant Young as he clung precariously to the ledge, the German raised his hands in a token of surrender.

'At the time I thought it was one of the funniest sights I had ever seen,' reported Lieutenant Young later, 'to see a German trying to scramble up a cliff with his hands up!'

Off-shore, the naval relief craft awaited with impatience and apprehension. No word had been received from the land forces due to the failure of the transmitting equipment and German patrol vessels were in the vicinity. It had been arranged that, as a last resort, Major Frost would fire off red Very lights, first to the north, then to the south of their position on the beach. This he did several times, without so much as a blink from off-shore. With a sinking heart he prepared to consolidate the position of his men in the full knowledge that the German garrisons within miles around had now been alerted to the raid.

Hardly had his men taken up their positions when a cry was heard.

'Sir, the boats are coming in! They're here! The Navy's here!'

The relieving party of Royal Fusiliers and South Wales Borderers which accompanied the landing craft directed heavy fire on the cliffs, as instructed. Only with difficulty were they persuaded to desist. The noise was deafening.

Major Frost saw all six landing craft approach the beach together. The orderly retreat which had been planned and rehearsed so many times in the bitter cold of Scottish lochs had to go by the board. The wounded and the captured radar equipment were top priority and these Major Frost organised into the leading landing craft. After that, it was every man for himself. They lost no time. Grenades and mortar bombs were beginning to make the beach untenable. The raiding forces were taken from the landing craft into the fast gunboats and made off for England with the landing craft in tow. Fighter cover was provided by the Royal Air Force and the men could breathe again. Major Frost and his men were later to learn the reason for his last resort Very pistols not being recognised by the Navy. A German destroyer and two E-Boats had passed by less than a mile away and, 'by the grace of God, had failed to notice us'.

Approaching Plymouth, as the raiding forces were taken towards the harbour, destroyers of the Royal Navy swung past at high speed to salute them. Wing Commander Pickard and his Whitley crews were on board to greet them. In the evening, to celebrate, an inter service party was held in the Naval Mess at Plymouth. It was an imperial party which ended in monumental headaches. The mission was complete.

For his operation Pick was awarded the first bar to his DSO.

The following day, under the heading 'Led Bombers on Bruneval Raid', the Press reported ...

> Wing Commander P. Charles Pickard, the DSO, DFC hero pilot, 'F for Freddie', in the film *Target for To-night*, led the carrying squadrons of RAF bombers which took the parachutist

force across the channel to their objective, the German radio location unit at Bruneval.

He is 26 years of age and the younger son of Mrs Pickard and the late Mr Percy Pickard, formerly of Hampstead, London, and Sheffield. Educated at Framlingham School, Suffolk, Wing Commander Pickard joined the RAF in 1936. He has had many adventures in real life, far more thrilling than those depicted in the film. One, with other members of his plane's crew, he spent 14 hours in a rubber dinghy, and began operations when the Germans went to Norway, and was also fighting in the air at Dunkirk.

Ming, an English sheepdog, is his constant companion and waits anxiously for his master's return from operational flights.

Mrs Pickard's elder son is Wing Commander W J Pickard who is in Canada. One of her daughters is Helena Pickard, actress wife of Sir Cedric Hardwicke. Her other two daughters, Marjorie and Nancy, have taken up work of national importance. On Monday a telegram of congratulations, handed in at Toronto, Canada, was received by Mrs Pickard from her son Walter and Sir Cedric and Lady Hardwicke, who are working hard in Canada for British and American War Relief Funds.

Returned to RAF Dishforth, Charles Pickard and his squadron received a request from Their Majesties King George and Queen Elizabeth. The Royal Family would like to see a practice drop made by the men involved in the Bruneval raid. Panic stations immediately! The last man to panic was Charles Pickard and organisation for the drop was undertaken with the same sense of unperturbed efficiency which had already characterised his attitude towards an increasing variety of operations.

It was arranged that all the Whitleys with their sticks of airborne troops would be in the air at the time appointed for the arrival of the Royal Family. The signal for the first aircraft to approach the airfield would be the approach of the Royal car at the guard room. When the Royal car appeared close to the guard room, the first Whitley would make ready for its dropping run, by which time King George and Queen Elizabeth could be counted upon to be on the tarmac. The Royal car drove towards the guard room, the Whitleys circled above, and King George expressed a desire to inspect the guard room and talk to the highly polished, nervous guards.

This unexpected delay was not anticipated by Pick, and he sent the first Whitley in for its dropping run. Ten of his aircraft followed suit, with the timing of a guardsman on parade.

With the King and Queen absent from the tarmac, the operation was going slightly hay-wire. A message from ground control was urgently sent out to Pick and his only other Whitley remaining in the air. A mild flutter of dismay, disappointment and panic was evident among the organisation on the ground at the late arrival of Their Majesties.

'Ground control to flight leader. Negative further drop. Royal party delayed. Please circle until further instructions.'

With most of the paratroops already on the ground and picking up their parachutes, the slick precision of the drop à la Bruneval, under a lesser mortal might have given rise to expletives, not necessarily of a Royal nature. Without a trace of alarm or disappointment, Pickard replied, 'Flight leader to ground control. Message received and understood. Wilco. Out.'

The Whitleys continued to circle until the King and Queen had been escorted to their seats, and the explanation given for the reduced number of aircraft on the circuit. Finally both aircraft made their dropping runs successfully but twenty men dropping accurately was a poor substitute for the full complement of 120 and the gist of the exercise lacked impact and was lost.

After being shown over the station and inspecting the airborne and Royal Air Force personnel, the King and Queen were invited to the Officers' mess for lunch. The mess had been cleaned to perfection and shone like a new button, except for one grievous oversight on the ceiling in the lounge. Leading from the entrance door of the lounge to the centre, a line of very distinct black footprints could be clearly seen. His Majesty King George turned to Charles Pickard and asked.

'Is there any significance in your ceiling decoration?'

'Well, no Sir,' fumbled Pick, 'I'm afraid it is the result of our mess party to celebrate our return from Bruneval. During the height of the proceedings, my shoes were removed, my feet were blackened with boot polish, tables and chairs were stacked on each other and I was perched at the top making footprints, as you can see. I am sorry, Sir.'

They walked into the mess, following the long line of footprints. At the end, and in the centre of the mess, there were two rather large blobs. Again His Majesty turned to Pickard for an explanation. It was time for Pick to really fumble for words.

'Well, eh Sir, I regret to say that those are the marks of my bottom!'

His Majesty laughed.

In the common room at Framlingham College, the pupils were gathered round the radio, listening to the latest war news which, at that time, was never far from bleak. Headlining the news was the raid on Bruneval, the first really successful combined operation of the war. Suddenly a shout went up from the boys as they clustered round the wireless set. The news flashed round the school.

'F for Freddie' had led the aircraft in the parachute raid on Bruneval!

'The best news all term,' shouted the boys. They were hoping for a holiday as when 'F for Freddie' won his DFC and DSO.

The head of the school, Mr R Kirkman, chuckled as he watched the boys listening to a description of 'Freddie's' run-in to the target area. He chuckled again when the press telephoned to ask him if he intended to allow the boys to celebrate another holiday.

'I expect so,' he replied, 'but in fairness to the boys, I must say they are more delighted at the Wing Commander's exploit than over the fact that it may mean a day's holiday. It was a fine piece of work, and we are all very proud of him.'

Three DSO's and one DFC later, the pupils at his old school of Framlingham were to celebrate the awards with four separate holidays. The procession of holidays at Framlingham were only matched by the visits to Buckingham Palace where the honours were bestowed.

The self-effacing and unassuming nature of the man was adequately demonstrated shortly after the Bruneval raid. He was invited to attend an Air Training Corps display at the Royal Opera House, Covent Garden.

Inspecting the cadets, soon to complement the ranks of the Royal Air Force, he asked Cadet Shorthouse of No 382 ATC Squadron what he intended to be in the Royal Air Force. The boy replied that he did not think that he was brainy enough to be a bomber pilot, although he would like to be one, and he would have to be an air gunner instead.

'But you don't need brains to be a bomber pilot!' replied Pick with a disarming smile, putting the young, keen cadet immediately at his ease. It was, perhaps, one of the understatements of the year.

CHAPTER SIX

Tempsford

Clandestine operations as a modus operandi in wartime are probably as old as war itself. Such operations are not considered with the respectability of orthodox warfare, but war, in any shape or form can hardly be considered respectable, and those involved in subversion are generally motivated by patriotism with the means justifying the end.

In 1938, the days of irregular warfare were considered past. No organisation for conducting it survived, no hard and fast rules existed and there was an abysmal shortage of trained operators in this field. One of the last irregular British armed offensives was conducted by the legendary Lawrence of Arabia but he had died accidentally in 1935. Some of his contemporaries had survived, but all were over forty-five and Britain was concerned with a new type of warfare in which aircraft would play a major part.

By June of 1939 a conclusion was reached that 'if guerrilla warfare is co-ordinated and also related to main operations, it should, in favourable circumstances, cause such a diversion of enemy strength as eventually to present decisive opportunities to the main forces.'

Any departure from tradition in the formation of a new unit was bound to meet with opposition from the hidebound directorate of military operations which was gagged by the blinkers of King's Regulations and Army Council Instructions, both unwieldy bodies and neither prone to a change from tradition. Fortunately, in the desperate summer of 1940, the politicians had the last say and Winston Churchill was looming large in the inept wake of Neville Chamberlain. Hugh Dalton was Minister of Economic Warfare and he attended a meeting called by Lord Halifax at a room in the Foreign Office on 1st July.

The following day Dalton wrote to Lord Halifax:

We have got to organise movements in enemy occupied territory comparable to the Sinn Fein movement in Ireland, to the Chinese guerrillas now operating against Japan, to the Spanish Irregulars who played a notable part in Wellington's campaign or – one might as well admit it – to the organisations which the Nazis themselves have developed so remarkably in almost every country in the world. This 'democratic international' must use many different methods, including industrial and military sabotage, labour agitation and strikes, continuous propaganda, terrorist acts against traitors and German leaders, boycotts and riots.

It is quite clear to me that an organisation on this scale and of this character is not something which can be handled by the ordinary departmental machinery of either the British Civil Service or the British military machine.

What is needed is a new organisation to co-ordinate, inspire, control and assist the nationals of the oppressed countries who must themselves be the direct participants. We need absolute secrecy, a certain fanatical enthusiasm, willingness to work with people of different nationalities, and complete political reliability. Some of these qualities are certainly to be found in some military officers and, if such men are available, they should undoubtedly be used. But the organisation should, in my view, be entirely independent of the War Office machine.

Halifax saw the Prime Minister and Churchill agreed to go ahead. On 16th July 1940, Winston Churchill invited Dalton to take charge of subversion, and with this invitation, Special Operations Executive (SOE) was born.

The work of SOE was in no way connected with espionage. Sabotage was its principal purpose; destroying of troop trains and VIG's (very important Germans), the collecting of guns, explosives and equipment to be on hand when the Allies returned to France, and efficiently slowing down the Nazis' war effort by dropping the odd monkey wrench into the gear box. In pilots and agents, it required a special kind of courage. They were on their own.

Of RAF Tempsford, a personal friend of mine, Eric Burke of Luton, has written the following poem:

Tempsford

In fleeting, darkened hours they met
By purpose joined together,
With but a word, or nod, and yet –
Their spirits linked forever.

Briefly their lives, the flyers and the 'Joes'
Were touched; no drums were rolled
Of men, and women, there were those
For whom the bells were tolled.

They have no shrine but in the heart
Of those of us who care –
To stand at Tempsford, and hear the start
Of engines, and of voices, in the air.

The 'Joes' referred to are the agents for France, Holland and Norway who rarely became known to the pilot or crew flying them. All had code names but, regrettably, not all were one hundred percent loyal either to their own country, or to Britain.

Top secrets of the war are not released until at least thirty years after the event and it is only now that names can be made known and incidents of the time released in the story of Charles Pickard.

Tempsford lies in a comparatively remote part of the Bedfordshire countryside. It is, as yet, unscarred by motorway or housing estates. The London to Edinburgh railway line runs close by and nearer still, a quiet country road, with neither giving a hint of an airfield within a stone's throw.

To-day, many of the old buildings and structures lie derelict, pointing their broken walls to the sky. An intangible atmosphere is strangely preserved from the limitless spirits of the past. The cracked and crumbled perimeter track lures the casual and observant visitor, with a compulsion to follow it across the fields until, with little previous hint of drama, unexpectedly and unmistakably, the old width of runway is revealed.

It is a strange paradox of nature that the very silence triggers a symphonic chord in the imagination. The imagination is fired by the rumble of a taxying aircraft, exhaust stubs glowing, lights blinking in the dark, and the green or red flash of an aldis lamp in the distance. The sounds and imaginative sights die away as one becomes aware of a group of buildings nearby, dwarfed to a certain extent by a large barn which has very obviously seen better days. Closer inspection of the large barn walls reveals an unkempt plaque bearing the legend 'Tempsford Airfield, Gibraltar Farm'.

Erected to commemorate the brave deeds of the men and women of every nationality who flew from this wartime airfield to the forces of the Resistance in France, Norway, Holland and other countries during the years 1942 – 1945. The equipment for their dangerous missions was issued to them from this barn.

A few paces away are the shells of two cottages to which the 'Joes' were brought and fed before receiving last minute instructions. In these derelict cottages the 'Joes' spent their last hours or minutes prepared and awaiting for what one of them (Wing Commander Yeo Thomas of *The White Rabbit* fame) was pleased to call 'the right kind of nights' until they boarded the aircraft waiting to take them to the 'wrong kind of nights'. Before boarding, if they had time to pause and reflect, the picture was one of a flat, green and wholly pastoral landscape stretching into the distance, soft and soothing. To the east rose a slight escarpment adding comfortably to the feeling of seclusion, so much in keeping with their desperate missions. Tempsford.

By virtue of the nature of public morale, the raids undertaken by Bomber Command made daily headlines. The Ruhr, Bremen, Hamburg, Hanover and countless others became well known to the embattled people of Britain. The deepening interest lay, not in the names of remote German cities under bombardment, but in the number of British aircraft which 'failed to return'. Of those engaged from RAF Tempsford, never a word was spoken, with each mission clouded in absolute secrecy and the pilots, crew (if any) and the Joes setting out into the complete unknown, steeped in unqualified danger. Bravery is a unique quality. Treachery is another colour. The personnel at Tempsford were to become acquainted with both.

RAF Tempsford was composed of two squadrons, No 138 which moved from Stradishall to Tempsford in March of 1942 and No 161 which moved from Gravely to Tempsford in April of 1942. Wing Commander Walter R Farley, the first CO of No 138 Squadron, Tempsford, was posted missing on the 20th April 1942, on a flight over Europe. Wing Commander F H Fielden commanded No 161 Squadron until he became CO of Tempsford in October of 1942. For some odd reason, Edward Fielden was known as 'Mouse' Fielden to his contemporaries, and remains so to this day. He was famous also as the Commanding Officer of the King's Flight. Wing Commander 'Mouse' Fielden was succeeded in the command of No 161 Squadron by Wing Commander Charles Pickard and in May 1943, who after having carried out over 100 sorties was promoted to Group Captain and handed over to Wing Commander I M Hodges. In 1944 No 161 Squadron was handed over to Wing Commander A H C Boxer.

In the invaluable and highly dangerous work of the personnel at RAF Tempsford, we must not forget the work of the Polish pilots and crews who moved with No 138 Squadron to Tempsford in March of 1942. Other Polish crews joined the squadron in 1942 and early 1943. In July of 1943 the Polish unit at Tempsford became known as No 301 Polish Flight under the command of Wing Commander S. Krol. Towards the end of 1943 No 301 Polish Flight moved from Tempsford to Tunis, and thence to Brindisi a few days later.

Poland has always been a proud, hard working and aristocratic nation and their country had been sadly and severely mauled by both Germans and Russians. With fanatical hatred against both the Nazis and the Communists alike, their every action on the ground or in the air abounded with a burning and fierce determination to do everything possible to restore freedom of thought and liberty of movement. With the Poles there were no half measures.

The personnel at Tempsford, air crew and ground staff, were a breed apart. Hand picked for their individual ability, whether on the ground or in the air, the airfield became a self reliant team of experts in their various fields. The pilots in particular were all of an 'Above Average' rating, and self reliance in navigation was equally, if not more, important. Particularly in the slow flying, low landing speed Lysander, the pilot was a man for all seasons. He had to fly across occupied enemy territory in the middle of the night, frequently in weather which grounded other squadrons, and navigate by himself to a certain field on a farm in the middle of France, Holland, or wherever. Once over the area which he considered to be the landing zone, the aircraft awaited a few brief flashes of a code which was the particular order of the day.

The landing 'grounds' were no more than that. It was a field on a remote farm which the underground considered suitable for the landing and take off, all of which had to be carried out in a matter of minutes. Whenever possible, the men from Tempsford would await a period of the moon which always gave them help in navigation, landing and take-offs. For this reason the pilots earned the name of the 'Moon Men' and the units to which they belonged, the 'Moon Squadrons'. Comparisons are at all times totally invidious, but one must hand a special bouquet to those involved in the delivery and removal of special agents who formed the basis of the underground movements. No 138 Squadron flew Whitleys, Lysanders and Halifaxes. No 161 Squadron flew Havocs, Hudsons, Lysanders, Halifaxes and Whitleys.

Between April, 1942, and May, 1945, some 29,000 containers, each holding 220 lbs of stores, 10,000 packages and 1,000 highly qualified agents were delivered to France and other European countries. Among the great variety of stores dropped were propaganda leaflets, food, clothing, radio equipment, medicines, sun-glasses, skis, explosives, and on one occasion 200 bottles of printers' ink, without a bottle being broken.

The bare statistics are only of academic interest. Those concerned, the secret agents, pilots and aircrews, performed and operated under the most appallingly dangerous conditions. When an agent was caught – as many were – interrogation by the Nazis generally concluded with unspeakable tortures, as in the case of Odette Churchill and Wing Commander Yeo Thomas, to mention two of the better known whose stories have been written. The final destination of those who survived these interrogations was the ultimate in degradation and savagery within the confines of a concentrations camp.

The agents working out of Tempsford conducted a private war of their own against the enemy which was fraught with danger and disaster. Their job involved the destruction of German installations which, by their very nature, were the most closely guarded. Railway lines carrying train loads of German troops had to be sabotaged at a precise moment to attain the greatest possible damage to the enemy, and information of troop movements and dispositions had to be fed back to London. This private war required highly trained, dedicated men and women whose exploits were never sung and whose future, if caught, at best ended in a merciful bullet and at worst, torture before being consigned to a concentration camp where few survived.

The Germans were fully aware of the agents being taken to France on individual flights to be dropped by parachute accompanied by canisters of various implements of destruction, or so be landed by smaller aircraft in a remote farmer's field for the same purpose while the aircraft picked up different agents who were returning to Britain with information required for some future operation. This particular type of operation was carried out in the very reliable, highly manoeuverable Lysander aircraft which had a very low stalling speed. Landing into a moderate wind, the Lysander could land and pull up in thirty-five yards. On such a mission, it was essential to land, taxi back to the landing point, empty the aircraft of the agent or agents with their paraphernalia, and pick up the returning agents, and be off, all within minutes. To help them in their landing, having flown and navigated the Lysander by themselves, a skeleton flare path was lit consisting of three ordinary torches!

The agents were trained in England how to select a suitable field for landing, smooth if possible, at least 150 yards in length and how to place the torches, mounted on sticks, into wind. The skeleton flare path was designed for easy installation and instant removal when the aircraft had left. The 'flare path' was in the form of the letter 'L' inverted. The first torch was placed at the bottom of the inverted letter 'L', sufficiently clear of hedges or trees on the approach for the landing of the Lysanders. 150 yards farther on the second torch was placed. At right angles and 50 yards away to the right of the second torch, the third torch was placed to indicate the end of the landing run. In common with the approach, the take off had to be clear of trees, hedges and telephone wires. The aircraft aimed to touch down as close as possible to the right of the first torch. Having landed, it carried on to swing round torch No 3, and return to torch No 1 as quickly as the ground conditions would allow. All ground control took place from torch No.1. When the sound of an approaching or circling aircraft was heard, 'ground control' would flash the necessary code letter for the day in the direction of the aircraft. In recognition, the aircraft would return the code letter required, and the 'flare path' was immediately lit. This, it must be remembered, all took place under the noses of the Germans and frequently in adverse weather conditions. Generally, and whenever possible, most of these operations were carried out during the period of a full moon which assisted the pilots in their very dicey navigation problems, and, as already mentioned, the crews involved were known as the 'Moon Men' attached to the 'Moon Squadrons'.

The 'ground control' and 'flare path' were almost laughable in their very simplicity but this simplest of means justified an efficient end, and it worked. Apart from the impossible weather under which these squadrons frequently worked throughout the winter periods, there was always the possibility that an agent had been captured, tortured, and forced to give the necessary information of an impending operation. If this happened, the aircraft, agents and pilots, would fly into the hands of the waiting Germans. It was not for the faint hearted.

Organisers in the underground were supposed to keep apart from their subordinates, who in turn were supposed to keep apart from each other. Defiance of such security training as they had received and any defiance of elementary prudence caused by the natural desire for companionship could cause an intelligible, pathetic error. For this, most of the agents would pay with their lives.

The amount of fore-thought and organisation required to send an agent into the field transcends the bounds of belief. Simple things, like clothing for instance.

Courtley Naismith Shaw is an illustrious sounding name. Less illustrious was the name given to this gentleman by the irreverence shown by his brother officers in the Royal Air Force. Taking their cue from the favourite tipple of Courtley Naismith Shaw, he was aptly described as 'Pink Gin Percy'. Whatever his shortcomings over a lunchtime session his work was of vital importance to the safety and survival of the numerous agents who passed through his hands. Courtley was in charge of equipping the agents both from Tempsford and from 138 Squadron at Huntingdon in clothing which would betray nothing of their origin in England. The equip-

Pickard at the time of the Bruneval raid.

Troops dashing ashore from landing craft.

One of the craft returning. Major J. D. Frost, who led the raid, is standing on the bridge, in front of the mast.

Pickard talking to paratroops who had dropped over Bruneval a few hours earlier

Their Majesties inspecting the paratroops after the raid

Their Majesties watch a demonstration. Major J. D. Frost is standing beside King George VI while Pickard explains a point to the Queen

ment was stowed in secret in an underground garage beneath Saville Row. It was part of a police station and the items of clothing were laid out on trestle tables.

There were suits for workmen, business men or professional men. Shirts and handkerchiefs were dubbed with the laundry marks of laundry establishments in Lille, Arles or Paris – wherever the agent would be operating, and if the agent was of the more humble workman type, he would be given a small fibre suitcase. The suitcase was filled with food for his lunch. French cigarettes, French matches and a French made flask for coffee or tea.

The cellar was also a veritable arsenal of Tommy guns, machine guns, and revolvers. The agents were issued with a fountain pen which contained a concealed but quickly accessible cyanide pill. These were used in cases of dire emergency or distress to enable the agents to forestall the agonies of torture and death.

Pink Gin Percy carried out one final act before the agents were flown from Tempsford to France. With meticulous attention to detail he would go over the individual agent with a very fine tooth comb to make absolutely certain that there was not a vestige of anything in the agent's clothing, parcels or suitcases which would connect with England thereby inviting possible disaster to the entire network in which the agent worked.

By his very nature, Pink Gin Percy was ideally suited for his job. As a guest in a home, he had the annoying and extraordinary habit of going round straightening any picture on the wall which was fractionally out of line. Having completed this regular chore, Courtley would run his finger along the window sill to check for dust. This odd performance which was a compulsion with the man earned him a low rating in the list of those who win friends and influence people.

Charles Pickard assumed command of No 161 Squadron at Tempsford in October of 1942. The policy and procedure for pick-ups had been more or less established by then. However, there could never be rigid rules over enemy territory as in the case of Bomber Command. Each pilot, on his individual flight, was bound to be presented by his own individual problems in weather, low cloud and fog, enemy action and the possibility of being ambushed after landing as the result of an agent being caught and tortured until the desired information was forthcoming. Initiative was at all times the byword of the moon squadrons. Into this might be written the favourite expression of Charles Pickard . . .

'There's always a bloody something!'

In his own experience, his favourite expression was to prove particularly apt.

The first three weeks of October 1942, saw little action from 161 Squadron as the weather had clamped down badly. Several flights had been organised but had to be cancelled at the last moment due to the weather. The night of 21st/22nd October was an improvement and three different operations were set in motion. 'Monkey Puzzle', with Wing Commander Pickard in Whitley Q 363; 'Periwig/Grantham' with Squadron Leader Gunn in Whitley R 6828 and 'Marrow', another Whitley commanded by Pilot Officer Foster. All had a crew complement of six, and the countries concerned were France, Belgium and Holland respectively.

'Monkey Puzzle' took off from Tempsford at 20.15 hours with four containers and five packets, heading for Tangmere in the South where the aircraft landed to top up on fuel. They left Tangmere at 21.11 hours, setting course at 3,000 feet to cross the Channel towards the French coast and passed their pinpoint of Cabourg at 21.54 hours. Holding to 5,000 feet they struck the river Loire four miles west of a group of islands east of Blois and ahead a bright light shone steadily in their direction.

Turning to make tracks for the light, it suddenly went out as the aircraft approached. They circled the position of the light until it suddenly came on again flashing the letter 'L' which was the code for the day and Pickard acknowledged the signal with a few brief flashes.

Immediately the remainder of the lights came on, and without further ado, the four containers were dropped from a height of 500 feet as they flew on a south-east course. Due to a misconception, the packages were not dropped on the target as they were thought to belong to the 'Grantham' aircraft and these they dropped at Marchenoir. There was neither sight of fighters or of the equally disturbing searchlights which invariably heralded an attack by enemy aircraft directing them to their target. Without further delay, course was set for home, crossing the French coast at Cabourg at 00.44 hours and base was reached at 02.45 hours.

The Whitley piloted by Squadron Leader Gunn had an equally incident free trip and succeeded in dropping six containers and six food packages from a height of 400 feet at Lessiers in Belgium before returning via Guise and crossing the coast at Haute-Banc at 1 500 feet. Base was reached at 01.25 hours.

'Marrow 4' had less success with Pilot Officer Foster in charge. 'Marrow 4' had set off from Tempsford at 21.37 hours with six containers and several packages of propaganda leaflets which were carried by most aircraft. The target area was in the vicinity of Kampen, in Holland, but no reception nor recognition could be made in the reception area and, apart from dropping the leaflets, 'Marrow 4' had to be content with an abortive mission and return to base with the six invaluable containers, landing at 03.40 hours.

There were several factors against the dropping of containers or packages, all of which contained the material necessary to continue the sabotage work against the enemy. Mainly the weather was liable to clamp down or the agents waiting at the other end had the misfortune of having a few Germans in the wrong place at the wrong time.

The work of the agents in the occupied territories was dangerous in the extreme with little hope of survival if caught in the act. This degree of danger was shared only by the aircrews flying the material into the danger zones and by the pilots of the Lysanders who had to make a landing and take off in enemy occupied land, always with the possibility of their mission and place of arrival being known to the Germans. Added to these ominous hazards, fighters on patrol on a moon-lit night had the advantage of being vectored on to the Allied aircraft with the help of search lights, or radar.

After several operations throughout October and the beginning of November, Charles Pickard set off in Lysander 'B' with one passenger and several packages for France. His passenger had made numerous trips back and forth and had become well known to both Pick and his wife, Dorothy; so much so that Monsieur Déricourt, as he was known to Pick and his wife, would be entertained to drinks and dinner before setting off in the middle of the night to his homeland of France on another cloak and dagger mission.

On 22nd November Pick, with one passenger aboard, set off at midnight for the Rouen area. The flight to France passed without incident, the target area was found without difficulty, and the Lysander landed to drop the one and pick up another waiting passenger for the flight back to England. The landing and take off operation was carried out in a matter of three or four minutes. The Lysander climbed quickly and was soon above a layer of cloud which helped to blot out their progress from any prying searchlights. It was a clear moonlit night above the clouds.

Levelling off at 3,000 feet above the cloud layer, they were crossing the French coastline, 'stooging along' in the language of the nonchalant, when the Lysander was presented with two German fighter aircraft making a head-on attack and another firing from behind on their starboard quarter. Pick had to act quickly. The German fighters had the Lysander on toast, with their infinitely greater speed, and the odds against the Lysander of three to one were definitely on the poor side. In favour of the Lysander was its much greater manoeuverability and on this Charles Pickard held his hand until the head-on fighters came within firing range. He whipped back the control column, shot straight up, and hung on the propeller as the offending aircraft swept fast underneath. Before they had time to make a wide turn due to their speed, Pick banged the rudder bar to port and the Lysander fell from her stalling point straight into a spin. The spin was maintained until cloud level was reached where the aircraft was levelled off with the appropriate action.

The fighters were not to be easily shaken off and they followed the Lysander into and through the cloud cover, firing as soon as the Lysander came within range. The position was not healthy. Pulling back heavily on the control column once more, the Lysander reared above cloud cover, stalled, and Pick threw his aircraft at once into a steep dive, through the cloud layer and held his dive straight for the sea beneath. At sea level, and with the wings reaching breaking point, he eased off, keeping a sharp look-out for another attack from behind, and called for fighter support on his radio. The fighters once more closed in with their superior speed from behind, and Pick waited until the last moment before standing on his wing and turning well inside the German fighters.

Tempsford

The cat and mouse game began to build up in favour of the Lysander as they approached the English coastline with the Germans fully aware that the Lysander had put out a distress call. They obviously had little heart for a confrontation with British fighters which would now be on their way, and they turned for home, high-tailing it at sea level. The Lysander climbed back into cloud and reached base at 04.40. The flight out and back, the antics with the German fighters and the excessive use of full throttle had taken their toll. The aircraft left Tempsford with 215 gallons of fuel on board. It landed with five.

Over a beer in the mess, when advised of the actual amount of fuel left in the tanks, Pick raised his glass and replied, 'Cheers! It's a long way to Tipperary!'

Towards the end of November special arrangements were made to carry out a joint operation known by the code name of 'Skate/Squid'. It was a masterpiece of close co-operation. The area concerned was Chateauroux, five miles south of Vatan. Flight Lieutenant Bridger, in Lysander GV 9353 left Tempsford at 21.15 hours with two passengers and six packages. As the return flight involved three passengers with luggage, it was necessary to send an extra Lysander. Pick left Tempsford simultaneously in BV 9367.

Although Flight Lieutenant Bridger was carrying two passengers plus packages, he arrived over the rendezvous at 23.20 hours which was fifteen minutes before zero hour. He decided to patrol the vicinity at 4 500 feet, calling Wing Commander Pickard on the RT every few minutes. In view of the hostile ears listening below, this was a practice not to be encouraged. However, after eight minutes he received a reply ordering him to proceed and land. Flight Lieutenant Bridger landed at 23.28 hours, the two passengers nipped out with eager hands helping them to remove the packages.

As the two returning passengers with their luggage were being loaded, Pick arrived overhead and Flight Lieutenant Bridger gave him a description of the field surface by RT. At 23.32 hours Flight Lieutenant Bridger took off, a matter of four minutes to de-plane two passengers plus packages and load up two passengers and their baggage. Silence having been broken, the possibility of the enemy reaching the scene with immodest haste occurred to Pick.

As Bridger took off, Pick landed and jumped on the brakes. He did not trouble to circle the third light. His waiting passenger ran to the aircraft, scrambled inside, and the Lysander was in the air within two minutes of landing. It was easier for Pick to handle Germans in the air than on the ground. He arrived back at Tempsford at 00.50 – five minutes after GV 9353. The entire operation of landing two agents with their packages and emplaning three others, in two different aircraft, had taken a total of six minutes on the ground. Contemporary airlines, please note!

The log reads, 'The flare path was excellently laid from south-west to north-east and the whole operation was carried through without a hitch.'

The months of November and December of 1942 were marred for operational flying from Tempsford due to the adverse weather conditions and several of the flights which were attempted became abortive over the landing areas as low cloud prevented pin pointing of the reception committee. However, flying between Tempsford, Tangmere and St Eval continued almost daily for Charles Pickard in the hope that the weather across the channel might clear at any time.

In December of 1942 he managed to complete one trip successfully by taking two passengers and their luggage across to France on the 22nd and returning safely to land at Tangmere. At 16.00 hours, with Flying Officer Hodgkinson at the controls of a Blenheim, Pick was flown to Tangmere for an operation in a Lysander the same night.

Having been briefed at Tangmere on the latest weather conditions to be expected, he took off at 22.30 hours. The weather was bitterly cold and severe icing conditions could only be avoided by flying as low as possible. It was also necessary to avoid the known positions of the anti-aircraft guns and search lights.

Fortunately cloud conditions although low had numerous breaks which allowed him the best of two worlds, by being able to map read through the breaks in the clouds and still seek the safety of the clouds and continue flying on instruments. Reaching the landing area he quickly saw and acknowledged the identification signal, circled, landed, de-planed his passengers with their luggage and took on board some packages for the return flight, all within the space of four minutes. Five and a half hours after leaving Tangmere he was back, returning by the same route he had taken on the outward flight.

The following day he was flown back to Tempsford and he decided to celebrate the coming festivate season and three weeks well earned leave by taking up a Tiger Moth for 'local aerobatics!' As he had done in June and July 1941 when he had been on non-stop operations over Germany. Pick once more sought relief from the tensions of operational flying by throwing the sensitive Tiger Moth all over the sky. Here at least he was not bound to a straight and level course and could give vent to his irrepressible buoyancy and flying spirit with the abandon which was characteristic of all his actions.

The 'great bustling spirit' of Major Frost's chief pilot on the Bruneval raid and the instigator of the dark, boot polish footprints on the mess ceiling after the raid as remarked by His Majesty King George, found its greatest outlet in the sky when he 'slipped the surly bonds of earth and danced the skies on laughter – silvered wings'.

Throughout December and January, operational flying was reduced to a minimum in deference to the cold weather-man of winter. The frustration for Pick was only relieved by local flying and cross country flights. On these, his devoted Ming logged quite a few hours which were duly recorded in her private flying log book. It is a remarkable tribute to his complete adaptability that the aircraft changed almost daily from the Lysander to the Tiger Moth; the Oxford to the de Soto and the Hudson to the Blenheim.

At the same time, with Dorothy indisposed, Pick had to exercise the two horses daily and take Ming out for her early morning rabbit run. The invigorating morning air he loved and he was pleasurably killing two bricks with the one bird.

For Charles Pickard, the lull in the flying allowed him to carry out the work he most hated but which had to be done. He was not the sedentary type and office work he considered for the birds. Piles of routine reports had to be made out, documents sifted through, letters written to the bereaved and checks made on his pilots' log books. He was able to cope instantly and well with the flying log books of his pilots engaged as they were in some of the most difficult and dangerous operational work of the war. On his desk he had a sheaf of scrap paper. A cursory glance at the last date and entry was enough to satisfy him that the log books were being kept up to scratch. He would then insert a scrap of paper as a matter of routine on which he had written, 'Keep your log book tidy'. The entry covered the good, the bad and the indifferent. For those who had kept their log books in impeccable order, the note on the scrap of paper served as a compliment. For those whose log books were moderately chaotic, it gave a jolt and for those at the bottom of the list who didn't care, it made no difference in any case. The entry was sufficient to keep Pick happy. It gave each pilot the impression that his log book had been scanned. In his own heart of hearts he felt that the pilots had more to do than keeping their log books tidy.

Christmas of 1942 and three weeks' leave at the same time would be sufficient to send most men with three tours of operations behind them into a Merry Christmas and a Happy New Year without much worry. The age-old festivities of Christmas in that year held a certain reserve and a great deal of domestic worry for Pick. Dorothy was expecting their first child, and this was the main reason for leave being taken. Dorothy had saved up for a huge duck for Christmas which was duly prepared and completed with all the etceteras. She was thoroughly looking forward to having Christmas dinner alone with Pick and a quiet evening by the fireside, with the mellowing influence of some French precious wine brought over earlier in the year by their friend Déricourt. Pick had gone off to the mess for a few drinks, 'with the boys' but was considerate enough to return to the house in good time for the dinner Dorothy had prepared with such care. When Dorothy answered his knock, she was met by Pick and two Czech pilots he had met on his travels. The duck, Dorothy felt, would be enough for themselves with possibly a bit left over to last out the following week. With a heart as big as himself he had felt sorry for the two Czechs being so far from home on Christmas Day.

A few drinks later and the duck appeared on the table, sunny side up and looking quite browned off and delicious. As housewives will – and Dorothy was no exception – she apologised for the duck instead of a turkey and expressed the hope that it would be sufficient for all four. Pick had fewer illusions. Set to carve the duck, he grabbed the large knife and fork and set about the duck in no mean manner. He cut it into exactly four squares and handed each his adequate, if rough, portion. The Czechs were highly honoured and deeply grateful to be spending Christmas Day with their former CO and left well into the wee small hours having dined and wined liberally. A taxi was called to take them back to their station with Pick escorting them to the gate, all flying a bit left wing low.

The following week, Dorothy had more to think about than a left-over Christmas dinner. Their child was making ominous signs of arrival and on New Year's Day, young Nick Pickard entered a world which was being torn by strife. Still, Dorothy and Pick for the time being, were the happiest and proudest parents in the Royal Air Force. The occasion was certainly one for celebrating and in due course a party was organised in the mess to wet the head of Nicholas Pickard. Mess parties, in wartime, were seldom in the nature of cheese and wine parties, and the birth of a son and heir to the commanding officer of 161 Squadron was no exception. With Dorothy still in hospital recovering well and young Nick showing signs of the lustiness of his father, the party was held with Dorothy in absentia.

When Bacchus is present, restraint is at a premium and the young pent-up pilots and aircrews of 161 Squadron were off the hook for days on end due to the inclement weather of January. The party was a singular success. It would have caused the do-gooders in the 'thou shalt not drink' brigade to weep at the antics of the highly pressurised, up-tight operational staff in aircrew letting their undercarriages down with such glorious and carefree abandon. Regardless of the protestations of the odd do-gooder, none of whom had suffered the slings and arrows of outrageous fortune in the air, the party hit the roof and crowded the floor without neglecting the points in between.

One of the points in between consisted of a wooden beam running the length of the bar. Later in the evening it seemed a splendid idea for those rejoicing to cross the length of this beam by the unconventional method of hanging by their toes. For those who succeeded there was a rousing round of applause. Ignominious failure was greeted by hoots of laughter and derision. Half way across the beam, hanging by his toes, all six feet four of Charles Pickard could not maintain the beer which had run to his head. He collapsed on the floor with a resounding bump. Using his free arm to break the fall, the thumb on his left hand and wrist took the brunt of his weight and, with a barely audible crack, he found himself with one broken thumb.

The thumb required the attention of the hospital authorities who examined it, made an x-ray, and slapped it into a plaster cast. The pain and inconvenience did not deter him from visiting his wife and son in the maternity ward on the following day. Dorothy was concerned, suspecting that he may have suffered a flying accident.

'Nothing to worry about,' Pick reassured her, 'I fell down the steps of the air raid shelter!'

'That,' Dorothy remarked, 'is a lie. You have never been in an air raid shelter in your life!'

His leave came to an end on 24th January and an operation calling for a trip into the heart of France was scheduled for the night of the 26th. Still with his wrist in plaster, Pick put himself down for the trip. The operation, known as 'Atala' required one person, equipment and four suitcases to be flown out, returning with two personnel and seven suitcases. One of the two returning passengers was a VIP and it was for this reason that Pick decided to make the trip himself.

The landing area was near Issoudun, approximately 70 miles due south of Orleans. With his one passenger and equipment, he took off from Tangmere at 22.45 hours into conditions of dark and poor visibility. They crossed the French coast at Cabourg and managed to pinpoint their position at 00.30 hours as five miles east of Orleans. From here they steered a course for Vierzon Villa and at 01.30 hours Pick estimated that he was over his landing area. Great difficulty was found in picking out the actual landing field due to the dark and difficult conditions of visibility. Conscious of one of the passengers due to be picked up being of some importance, Pick remained and circled the area until 03.15 hours.

To circle an area of enemy territory for the best part of two hours at a fairly low altitude required nerves of steel, a very sharp look-out and an eye constantly on the petrol gauge. Flying with revs and throttle set for maximum endurance, the position was rapidly growing hopeless as the fuel gauge dropped lower and lower. Thoroughly disappointed, he was about to head for home when he saw a weak recognition light flashing.

He signalled back in acknowledgement and threw the aircraft into a dive for the recognition light. Wasting no time in landing nor in formalities, he had landed, rid himself of his passenger plus luggage and emplaned the two awaiting passengers with their seven suitcases all within the space of minutes.

He took off without delay, climbed slowly on course to conserve as much fuel as possible, and made for England. As they crossed the channel the fuel gauge was approaching a zero reading, and Pick was happy to make for the nearest possible landing ground. Approaching Predannack in Cornwall at 3,000 feet, the engine cut and he had no alternative to a forced landing. The time was 06.30 and he had been in the air for a total of seven hours and forty-five minutes.

Neither of his two French passengers were aware of the drama and tension experienced by Pick as he approached the English coastline with the fuel gauge running out and his successful forced landing without power moved them not a bit. Their main concern was trying to find out why he had circled the target area for such a long time without giving them the recognition signal. Due to a misunderstanding, the reception party had been waiting for the recognition signal to come from the Lysander first, before they replied. Tired of waiting, and as a last resort, they had decided to signal to Pick's aircraft. Back at Tangmere and after debriefing, they joined Pick for breakfast. Following the custom of all broken limbs surrounded by plaster casts, both signed their names. One of them was Monsieur René Massigli, former French Ambassador to Turkey.

The old, reliable, but slow flying Anson which had retrieved Wing Commander John Nesbitt-Dufort from France after his Lysander had become bogged down and conveniently written-off by the Paris express while being 'helped' across the line by members of the Resistance with the help of their unwelcome German masters, had established a precedent. This operation had proved that twin-engined aircraft, in the proper hands, could be used for the movement of the Underground personnel, to and from France. By February of 1943, Wing Commander Pickard began to make a more intimate acquaintance with the flying characteristics of the Hudson aircraft, better known for its performance as a medium bomber.

The French Underground had stepped up their sabotage efforts against the Germans by 1943 and many more agents became involved. Halifax bombers were still being used to drop men and supplies but the big Halifax was quite unsuitable for landing in a restricted area. It was essential to pick up as many Underground workers as possible from France, armed as they were with details of German troop and defence dispositions, and the requirements to destroy them.

On 1st February, Charles Pickard and Squadron Leader Hugh Verity took up Hudson 'O for Orange' for a period of one hour fifteen minutes to familiarise themselves with the controls and for the operations ahead. Squadron Leader Verity had been flying Lysanders with 161 Squadron for some time and had considerable experience of the routine and dangers involved. He had been asked to write up the fundamental rules of the game and this work became the standard procedure to be adopted for operations concerned with SOE. Apart from the cloak and dagger dangers involved in the landings and pick-ups of French agents, Verity had just completed a trip on the night of the 26th/27th January which had frustration to accompany the element of danger. It was the same night in which Pick ran out of petrol.

It was a double operation known as 'Prawn' and 'Gournal' with a third aircraft thrown in as 'Whitebait' for good measure and to cover any eventualities. The pilots concerned were Squadron Leader Verity, Flying Officer Rymills and Pilot Officer McCairns flying Lysanders with the appropriate markings of 'D', 'F' and 'C' respectively. The aircraft became airborne between 22.10 and 22.15 and after passing over the French coast, a re-call signal was sent out. Word had been received from their landing area that the ground was covered in fog. The only person to pick up the re-call message was Pilot Officer McCairns. Having acknowledged the message, he was asked to try and contact the other two aircraft, to advise them to return to base. In this he was unsuccessful and made an about turn for base on his own. The other two aircraft flew happily on, making their way on course to their target and contact between these two aircraft was made at 00.10 hours. Flying Officer Rymills arrived first on Target at 01.25 hours and found the target covered in a fairly low fog. The reception party had heard the approaching aircraft and switched on their elementary flare path when they considered the aircraft close enough to see it. By good fortune the lighting was bright enough to be seen through the fog and Flying Officer Rymills was able to land at 01.30 hours. His own passengers quickly disembarked and two more entered his aircraft for the return trip.

Overhead Squadron Leader Verity remained in the vicinity waiting for Rymills to complete his job. Rymills finally took off at 01.40 hours, set course immediately for the river Saone, at the same time giving Verity the all-clear to land. Hugh Verity landed into an inglorious mix-up. On the ground he found a party of no less than ten people, including the Mayor from the local village, and no passengers to pick up! By questioning the mob of Frenchmen on the airfield it quickly became apparent that they had been expecting only one aircraft and not a double operation with the result that only two agents had been organised for the return trip and both of these had gone off with Flying Officer Rymills. As no-one seemed to want a free flight to England, Squadron Leader Verity wasted no more time and set off in pursuit of Rymills. Both aircraft returned safely to base and landed almost simultaneously at 05.20 hours.

From 1st February until the 12th Wing Commander Pickard carried out a total of nine flights in Hudson 'O for Orange' with one flight in a Lysander on the 4th . . . 'just to keep his hand in'. These flights were mostly local, with the longest being to Kinloss and back. As an indication of his adaptability and experience in various types of aircraft, by the time he was called upon to undertake his first trip to France in a Hudson during the hours of darkness on the night of 13th February, he had a total of seven hours, daytime flying and forty-five minutes of night flying. His first Hudson trip to France by night was almost as long as his total Hudson experience combined.

The weather of February restricted operations severely and of the few carried out, 'three very notable and successful operations were carried out by Wing Commander Pickard', according to the station log book. The last of these so very nearly ended in disaster.

The first operation in Hudson 'O for Orange' by Charles Pickard took place on the night of 13th/14th February, 1943, and was known as operation 'Sirene Berenice'. The crew was restricted to Pilot Officer Taylor and Flying Officer Figg as their complement included five agents with their 'packages'. Their target area was St Yan twenty miles due north of Roanne, on the river Loire. Leaving Tempsford at 20.20 hours, they reached the French coast via Tangmere at 21.40 hours. At this hour they were over the river estuary west of Cherbourg. From here they set course to the islands east of Blois and made a slight alteration of course to Nevers where they were able to pick up the river Loire. The target was found without much difficulty by following the course of the river and a torch was seen flashing the letter 'N'. Pickard answered with an incorrect letter 'to see what would happen!' All lights on the ground were at once extinguished and they continued to circle the target area before giving the correct answering letter. In answer to his correct letter flashed to the ground, two red lights came on and some time elapsed before the flare path was laid out and fully lit. The reception party were still nervous of the approaching Hudson as it came in to land, believing that a trap might have been set by the Germans. They remained in the shadows and out of sight until the Hudson had landed and taxied back to its take-off point. Only by shouts and assurance from the five French passengers could they be persuaded to make an appearance and help out with the removal of the packages. The return load consisted of mail only and the operation, from time of landing until take-off was unduly protracted due to the nervousness of the local Underground workers in making their appearance. The delay did not worry Pick unduly. His purpose in sending out the wrong recognition letter was to make sure that the reception committee were on their toes! In this he had succeeded and he was at pains to congratulate them before taking off at 23.25 hours and following the same route, returning to base at 02.35 hours.

In the 1970's, and thirty years after the event, a flight of nine hours would not have the effect of raising an eyebrow. Within the week of purposely giving the wrong recognition signal, Pick was off again on the night of 20th/21st February with a crew of Pilot Officer Taylor as his navigator and Flying Officer Figg once more as the wireless operator. Their destination was Arles in the very south of France and for company they had only one passenger on the outward trip with his baggage. The main purpose of the operation was to pick up six agents at Arles with their luggage and return to England.

It was a very long haul over territory in the hands of the opposition, with searchlights and known gun emplacements to be avoided at all costs. Taking off from Tempsford at 19.00 hours, they again reached Cherbourg at a height of 8 000 feet, having flown via Tangmere. From Cherbourg they set course at 20.20 hours for the islands in the Loire east of Blois which by now had become well known and were easily recognisable by Pick and his aircrew. Flying on instruments and with the aid of 'George', the automatic pilot, course was set for Avignon, a cool 300 odd miles in a south easterly direction. They passed directly over Issoudun where an earlier pick-up had been made. In their navigation they had the comfort and help of knowing that the river Rhone with a railway line running close to the river lay on their port side. If in any doubt they had only to turn to port, find the river and follow its course to Avignon.

This was not necessary and in due course the area near Avignon was found by pin pointing on a canal. The recognition lights from the aircraft were put on at once, but the answering signal could not be observed. An emergency letter 'X' was signalled from the aircraft and the elementary flare path was immediately lit. On landing, which was done without further palaver, it was found that the battery in the hand torch was weak and their signal could not be observed from the air! Having flown from the south of England to the south of France and overcoming all the dangers which such a night flight entailed, the entire exercise might have been abandoned due to a weak battery in a hand torch.

The landing was completed without difficulty and the Hudson taxied back to the first landing light and the point of take-off. Their single passenger jumped out with his equipment and the six who were detailed for the pick-up scrambled on board. Behind them, their personal baggage was thrown aboard without ceremony. From landing, disembarking, embarking and take-off, the total time on the ground was seven minutes. This gave Charles Pickard just enough time to light his inevitable pipe and enjoy the sweet aroma before closing all doors and opening the taps for a take-off over a short space of ground better suited to the grazing of mountain goats.

One of his six passengers from Arles for the return flight was General de Lattre de Tassigny. In addition to signing the plaster cast on Pick's arm, General de Tassigny later signed the armistice agreement in Berlin on behalf of France.

Once airborne the crew of 'O for Orange' were in their own element, ready to cope with any emergency. The return journey was made by the same route and on the approach to England, a call was made from Tangmere, requesting them to divert and land at Tangmere as there was some doubt about the weather conditions at Tempsford. They remained at Tangmere for a period of only eight minutes before word came through that conditions at Tempsford appeared to be clearing. They took off immediately, heading for their home station and arrived to find that they had no difficulty in making the flare path and a perfect landing at 03.35 hours. The round trip of close on nine hours which had been fraught with danger throughout received the comment from Pick that 'everything went off smoothly and it was a piece of cake!'

Students of art throughout the world will associate Arles as being the home of Vincent van Gogh, the Dutch artist, for a time. In the last war, Special Operations Executive and the French Underground had other reasons to remember Arles.

Fifty miles south east of Arles lies the old port of Marseilles. The Reverend Donald Caskie had been called to the Scots Kirk in Paris from Gretna, a quiet country parish on the shores of the fast flowing Solway, in 1935 and had grown to love Paris, France and all its people. On a sunny Sabbath morning in 1940 he made his last wartime service from the pulpit of the Scots Kirk which had been in existence for nearly a century as the German army marched relentlessly towards Paris.

The service ended and outside he commended his people to God and bid them all au revoir. After days of walking, dodging the enemy aircraft as they strafed the marching columns without hindrance, he arrived exhausted at the port of Bayonne, close to the French/Spanish border.

As he walked through the port area, somehow, overwhelmingly, he became aware that he should remain in France. On the dockside, looking at the masses of badly wounded men he decided that he could not accept a passage. He felt that the sick and the grievously wounded had first priority which, to him, was their right. As the last ship steamed out of Bayonne, he watched it go.

By devious means he made his way to the port of Marseilles, where he felt sure he could lose himself in a hotch-potch of races, passing mariners, and a conglomeration of accents where his native Gaelic might serve him well to escape being understood.

Marseilles was in turmoil with the streets and docks crowded with British soldiers and airmen who had made their escape from Dunkirk. Most were in a pitiable state of exhaustion, undressed wounds and, to a man, starving. Donald Caskie decided to seek the help of the local police in an effort to find a suitable building to help accommodate those in need from his own part of the world. He was accompanied to the door and downstairs by another detective.

With their help he took over the British Seamen's Mission which was deserted.

The undercover work carried out by the Seamens' Mission in Marseilles during the war under almost impossible conditions of secrecy in returning British soldiers and airmen to Britain in civilian clothes is described at length in the book written by Donald Caskie, *The Tartan Pimpernel*. It touches upon the story of RAF Tempsford and Charles Pickard in particular.

The problems of feeding and clothing the increasing numbers who came his way harried the good padre no end. Everything required money and this was in extremely short supply.

Each cash crisis seemed to be resolved at the last moment by one of these casual callers until one day a visitor called to see the padre in the morning. He was a very charming person, but Donald Caskie had grown extremely wary of charming people.

'You need money, I know', began the visitor when they were safely within the confines of the Mission office, 'and I have brought you a little contribution.'

At first the padre was non-committal. In his best and strongest Scottish accent Donald Caskie replied, 'Have ye ever met the meenister yet who doesn't require money?'

His visitor laughed and Caskie felt slightly re-assured. His visitor placed a large package on the padre's desk and his next sentence put the mind of Donald Caskie at rest.

'Van Gogh has been very helpful.'

Donald Caskie knew that the reference to van Gogh was the town of Arles where the famous artist had lived and he also knew that the Royal Air Force were conducting a thriving, clandestine air service between Arles and England. When the name of van Gogh was mentioned, the Reverend Caskie felt more confident that his visitor was altogether bone fide.

His visitor rose to leave.

'Ah, our little contribution to your Mission, Monsieur le Pasteur. With it comes our good wishes and prayers', and with that he bowed himself out.

After he had gone, Donald Caskie sat for a long time in silent appreciation, looking at the parcel. He lifted the thick envelope which had been sealed with red wax and turned it upside down, having burst the seal. A fold of bank notes fell out, but there was no message. Mechanically he started to count out the notes. It was exactly £5000, in French currency. To the padre it represented a vast sum of money with which to carry on the good fight from his corner of a foreign field. The money itself was a monumental help to his Mission. Of even greater significance to Donald Caskie, if that were possible, lay in his appreciation that his efforts had filtered back to England, and his work was now being recognised by the British Government with the incalculable help of the Royal Air Force. The pilots from RAF Tempsford knew little of the work behind the men they flew back and forth. The less they knew the better. Donald Caskie and his Mission in Marseilles represented one source of information, agents and an added nail to the coffin of the Nazi war machine.

The life and the teaching of the pilots and aircrews from Tempsford and the life's work of Donald Caskie were worlds apart. As long as the war lasted they had one thing in common. Both were in the transport business. If Donald Caskie had reason to be grateful to the men from Tempsford for the superb gift of £5,000, at least one of those later at Tempsford had an equally good reason to be thankful for services rendered by the good minister of the Scots Kirk.

Wing Commander Lewis Hodges who was to assume command at Tempsford on the promotion of Charles Pickard, found himself in dire straits after the miracle of Dunkirk in 1940. For Lewis Hodges it was no miracle. He was left behind.

In the company of others suffering the same plight, he made his way to the south across France in the hope that refuge and repatriation could be effected by crossing into Spain.

So many were crowding into the Seamen's Mission and Donald Caskie was being kept so busy in the early days of 1940 that it was some time before he thought to question the soldiers and airmen as to how they had learned about him. They expressed surprise at his ignorance. British Intelligence in Northern France had instructed them to make for Marseilles, find the Seamen's Mission, and ask for Donald Caskie! The Reverend was not too sure that he was flattered by his activities and fame spreading so rapidly. More hostile ears might be listening. Lewis Hodges was packed off safely to England. Without any connection at this stage with Tempsford, it would seem that as the Reverend had sown, so did he reap.

The night of February 24th/25th, 1943, was a night of typical cold, sleet and snow in England. With most of the Bomber Command stations grounded due to the adverse conditions, it fell once more to the lot of RAF Tempsford to carry out a long and hazardous mission to the area of Tournais/Cuisery. A total of seven passengers had to be picked up and returned to England as these men were being closely pursued by the Gestapo and it was essential to get them back to the safety of England before the Gestapo pounced. Wing Commander Pickard elected to fly the Hudson 'O for Orange' himself as he felt that he knew the landing area better than the other pilots and conditions were such that they called for only the most experienced.

They set off from Tempsford at 22.27 hours with Pilot Officer Taylor navigating, Flying Officer Figg as the wireless operator and Flight Lieutenant Putt borrowed from 138 Squadron as second in command to Pick. The weather was grim but they managed to cross the coast west of Tangmere before striking the French coast near Cabourg at 23.51 hours. There was no improvement in the weather and they altered course on the Loire on their estimated time of arrival as thick fog prevented any visual pinpoints. The thick fog persisted until le Creusot where, for a short time, the weather cleared. Further on fog was again found in the target area which was reached at 01.30 hours, with conditions so appalling that Pick had to circle the landing area for two hours as he made about twenty attempts to get the aircraft down. Their greatest worry was circling round so often before landing which could only draw attention to the Hudson from hostile ears on the ground.

In the end, at 03.30 hours, with the ground and flare path barely visible, a desperate attempt at landing was made. Under the conditions in which they found themselves, the landing was heavy and made to the wrong side of the flare path. To add insult to injury, when they taxied to the end of the 'runway', the Hudson became bogged down. The position of the aircraft, crew, and the waiting agents was now truly perilous. The noise of the aircraft circling the local village for two solid hours had attracted the attention of some of the villagers who had turned out for the landing and had joined the agents. Between the bystanders, agents and the crew, the aircraft was dug out in half an hour and Pick taxied the aircraft as far back as he could for the take-off.

After about a quarter of a mile, the aircraft became bogged down for a second time and here hope was almost given up. To Flight Lieutenant Putt, Charles Pickard was later to make a special commendation for the manner in which he remained cool throughout the ordeal, organised the labour force which had by now grown considerably with, in his opinion, half the villagers digging, pushing and pulling, sided and abetted by one large grey horse. Fear and frenzy added to their efforts, but it still took a further hour and a half before the aircraft was in a position considered suitable by Pick for the beginning of the take-off run.

In the words of Pick's de-briefing report, 'it was very difficult to get any sense out of the French as to distances and the original flare path could not be located!'

The French talked in metres, while the aircrew talked in yards. Both added to the confusion of the distance to the nearest fences and trees at the end of the non-existent 'runway'. The Hudson was carefully taxied back as far as possible with the 'more intelligent Frenchmen' and the aircrew testing every yard of the way for soft ground. When Pick made up his mind that he should have sufficient clearance for the take-off, he emplaned his crew and the seven agents. The take-off was effected by guess and by God. In the darkness, without the aid of a flare path, Pick lined the aircraft up, set on his instruments and revved up the engines before releasing the brakes to trundle over the damnably yielding ground. He could only 'feel' the aircraft into the air, sweating it out that they would clear any obstructions at the end of their run.

Reluctantly the big Hudson became airborne, the first hurdle had been overcome and they started to climb as best they could. Out of the night, without any hope of recovery action, a large tree spread its menacing branches. It was impossible to ease back on the control column without inviting disaster.

The aircraft was already flying on the point of stall and not a further inch of lift could be asked of the labouring engines. Pick held straight to his course with no more than a hope and a prayer to help him. The leading edge and the wing tip struck the higher branches with no more damage than putting 'George', the automatic pilot, out of action. It was the understatement of the year when he described his brush with the tree as a 'lucky escape'. Course was set for base and the French coast was crossed north of le Havre at 07.03 hours. As dawn was now breaking, Pick sent out an emergency call for fighter protection. No fighter protection responded to his distress call and they eventually reached base at 08.00 hours.

The post-script to this operation underlines the miracle of their survival. 'On becoming airborne at 05.30 hours, it was thought that one or two cars could be seen approaching. *A very striking note in this operation was the fact of remaining unmolested by the Germans, as the fact of first making so many circuits before landing must have caused some attention.*'

This observation by Charles Pickard suggested no significance at the time. Later it assumed a more ominous ring.

Back home at Tempsford, Dorothy had been left alone with baby Nick and Ming when Pick took off at 10.30 for his trip to France. Dorothy had waited up to see Pick leave the house at 9 p.m. for the airport and the briefing room, before settling down for the night. With their child barely two months old, Dorothy had her own work cut out and the trip to France was merely another operation in her husband's life which had been both hectic and fully operational since the beginning of war. Before the Hudson had taken off for France, Dorothy had settled down for the night and was soon asleep.

At 01.30 hours, Ming wakened Dorothy by pulling on the blankets of the bed. The big English sheep dog had done this before, on the occasion when the aircraft Pick was flying had made a forced landing in the sea. Dorothy was awake at once, full of apprehension. She opened the front door to allow the dog the use of the garden, bitterly cold and covered in snow. Ming walked outside but made no effort to spend the proverbial penny. The dog looked up to the sky, to the right and to the left and, of a sudden, Dorothy knew that Pick was in trouble. Covered in her shaggy great coat, Ming did not seem to feel the effect of the cold. The dog remained outside in the cold, constantly looking up at the sky, to the right and to the left. No words of coaxing on the part of Dorothy would induce Ming to come into the house. She remained outside as Dorothy closed the door against the weather and returned to the lounge to make up the fire, brew a pot of tea, and wait out the night, fearful and in trepidation.

Outside, in the snow and the cold, Ming continued to look to the sky while Dorothy made the odd call to the ops room for word of 'O for Orange'. Oddly enough, it was more than three years before when Pick and his crew had force landed in the sea, in a Wellington, also under the code name of 'O for Orange'. The code name was growing ominous and monotonous. For obvious reasons there was no news of the Hudson over France and Dorothy had no alternative to leaving Ming out in the cold as the dog persisted in her refusal to come into the house. With a heart of lead, Dorothy waited up most of the night, sitting by the fire, hoping for the best but anticipating the worst.

It was a long and bitter night until precisely half past five in the morning. Shortly after the half hour struck on the clock, Dorothy heard a constant and loud scratching on the door. In a state of great trauma Dorothy moved to the door not knowing what to expect. Ming looked up at Dorothy as the door was opened, wagged her short tail, and swept past Dorothy towards the fireplace. Curling up in front of the fire, Ming was sound asleep in a matter of minutes, and Dorothy retired at once to bed. Now that Ming had returned and was sound asleep in the lounge by the fire, Dorothy knew that Pick was somehow, somewhere, on his way back. Shortly before 8 a.m. Dorothy was again awakened by Ming. Between Pick, the baby and the dog, Dorothy's hours were growing most irregular. She opened the door as Ming scurried out. Approaching the end of the runway a Hudson hove into sight. Dorothy watched out long enough to read the identification letters. They read 'O'. Pick was back.

This particular operation, carried out successfully in the most adverse of conditions, bogged down for four hours, hitting the tree on take-off and finally limping back to England without the fighter protection asked for, brought in its wake the third DSO to be awarded to Charles Pickard.

As usual, the presentation would be made at Buckingham Palace. Dorothy and Pick made their way to London to relax for a few days prior to the presentation. Several of his Air Force friends were in London for the same purpose. He invited them round to his hotel to celebrate on the eve of the presentation. The ale and the wine flowed freely. Tomorrow was another day. His left arm was now out of plaster though rather weak. This did not affect his good, strong, drinking arm and with Buckingham Palace on the morrow, party tricks were definitely out. The party continued well into the morning hours with the thought of Buckingham Palace growing more distant with each successive glass.

The day after the night before, Dorothy tried without success, to move Pick. No, he was not going anywhere, he mumbled, not even to Buckingham Palace. He was ill, thoroughly ill, and please would Dorothy telephone the Palace!

The impasse was broken by the arrival of his mother. Not having attended the party in his room, his mother was less understanding and a degree more forthright. She had Pick out of bed like a naughty schoolboy, hustled to bath and shave, and prepared suitably for the occasion. To his mother he was still very much a naughty schoolboy. It was the sort of morning when a pledge is made never to touch a drink again. Still protesting, Pick left for the Palace with his wife and his mother.

The presentation over, the guests, friends and dignataries took their leave.

'Feel like a hero?' asked Dorothy when they were outside.

'No!'

'What do you feel like?'

'I feel like a bloody good drink!'

Together the trio made for the nearest hotel to celebrate three DSO's.

Cables of congratulation arrived from old colleagues, relatives and friends. Among the cables was a letter which gave him great pleasure.

Headed 'Combined Operations Headquarters, 1a Richmond Terrace, Whitehall, S.W.1' and dated 1st April 1943, it read:

> Dear Pickard,
> I am writing on behalf of all your old colleagues at Combined Operations Headquarters to offer you our most sincere congratulations on getting a second bar to the DSO.
> What a very fine performance. We are all basking in your reflected glory.
> Yours sincerely,
> Louis Mountbatten.

It was particularly gratifying to be remembered by his comrades-in-arms as a whole who had been involved with him the previous year on the vital raid against Bruneval. Much publicity had been given to Bruneval. By the nature of his work out of Tempsford, none could be given to the bogged down trip to France.

It was an odd coincidence. All three DSO decorations had been earned in the months of February; the first in 1941 while with 311 (Czech) Squadron; the second on the Bruneval raid in Whitleys; and finally the Hudson trip to the area of Tournais/Cuisery which had so nearly ended in disaster. The first decoration of the DFC had been awarded during the time of the Norwegian campaign in the early days of the way. Pick now became the first man in World War Two to have been awarded three DSOs in the same war, in the air. It was an enviable record, befitting one with the relentless compulsion to drive himself to the extreme on operations. This is best summed up in summary of events of 161 Squadron for the month of February, 1943:

Except for three very notable and successful operations carried out by Wing Commander Pickard in the Hudson aircraft, very few operations were able to be carried out. This was again largely due to weather conditions.

The aeronautical correspondent of *The Times* was more explicit. Under the heading, 'Third DSO for Wing Commander Pickard', the citation and comment reads:

> This officer has completed a very large number of operational missions and achieved much success. By his outstanding leadership, ability, and fine fighting qualities, he has contributed in a large measure to the high standard of morale of the squadron he commands. Wing Commander Pickard, famous as the pilot of 'F' for 'Freddie' in the film *Target for To-night*, has set up a new record by being the first airman to be awarded the DSO three times in one war.* Group Captain Basil Embry also holds the DSO and two Bars, but his original award was made for activities on the North West Frontier before the war.
>
> Wing Commander Pickard, who is the Commanding Officer of No 161 Squadron, carried the parachute troops employed in the attack on Bruneval in February 1942, and when he was awarded a first Bar to his DSO for this and other work, the citation concluded with this exceptional tribute: 'by his courage, self-sacrifice, and devotion to duty, this officer has set an example which, although attained by few, is admired by all'.

Unknown to most, and one which had received much less publicity, was the additional award of the Czechoslovak Military Cross of 1939.

Deservedly, the heroic efforts of all the Hudson crew in battling with the mud and against time on the night of 25th February received recognition. Flying Officer Dickie Taylor, RCAF, 161 Squadron, Flying Office H R Figg and Flight Lieutenant A J Putt all received the DFC. Sadly for Dickie Taylor, by the time the awards were made known, he had been reported as missing.

The headmaster at Framlingham College, Pick's old beloved school, was not slow to recognise his former pupil's mounting dis-

---

* Albert Ball VC, DSO, MC, had achieved this in 1916.

tinction. For the third time the pupils at Framlingham enjoyed an extra school holiday.

The clandestine story of Tempsford would be incomplete without reference to the night of 16th/17th December 1943, when Wing Commander Hodges was in charge of 161 Squadron, and Pick had been promoted to Group Captain and transferred. In December of 1943 Pick was the Officer Commanding 140 Wing in 2 Group of the Tactical Air Force in yet another operational role.

Tempsford had its frequent moments, but none so desperate as the night of 16th/17th December of 1943. It was perhaps the most disastrous night in the history of the station. Ironically, none of the events were caused by enemy action.

Flight Lieutenant Robin Hooper was one of the Lysander pilots at Tempsford. During the moon period of November 1943, he had made a flight to France, under the code name of 'Operation Scenery I' to Poitiers in the south-west. Conditions at the landing field near Poitiers were far from suitable, even for a comparatively light aircraft, and the Lysander became bogged down. It was believed, and hoped, that Hooper had succeeded in setting fire to his aircraft to prevent it falling into the hands of the Germans.

Word came back to Tempsford through the Underground in the area that Robin Hooper was safe and he had gone into hiding. It was decided to launch 'Operation Scenery II' to pick him up. Further details of his exact location, the organisation of a suitable landing strip, and numerous other details had to be worked out before the attempt to retrieve Robin Hooper could be made. By the time all details had been worked out the full benefit of the moon period in November had passed. The rescue operation would have to wait until the following month.

Wing Commander Hodges decided to undertake the rescue operation himself. A new radar navigational aid known as GEE was a device which had been developed for Bomber Command in 1942. It provided an accurate means of navigation over Europe within a range of 200 to 300 miles from Britain. Wing Commander Hodges had the idea of fitting a GEE set to his Lysander, which, coupled with the assistance of his own navigator, Squadron Leader Wagland, would give them the maximum chance of success. It would be a long and dangerous trip over enemy territory and the weather of December in Europe can be accounted as unpredictable as a Scottish summer. Flying at a low altitude, it was assumed that the GEE set would provide assistance at least to the Loire and this would be invaluable. The success of the trip was most important. Lewis Hodges well remembers the commanding officer at Tempsford, Mouse Fielden, saying . . . 'Be careful. We don't want to have to lay on "Scenery III!" '

With time available before the next moon period of December, it was hoped that the necessary modifications required to install the GEE set in the Lysander would be complete. It was also imperative to carry out trials in the air, and for this Squadron Leader Wagland accompanied Wing Commander Hodges. Everything seemed to be working well and they stood by, waiting for the next moon.

The first attempt on 'Operation Scenery II' was made on the night of 15th/16th December. The Lysander took off from Tangmere and followed their usual route. It soon became apparent that the GEE set was giving large compass fluctuations and these had not shown up in the course of the trials. Worse was to follow, and between the coast of Normandy and the Loire they ran into foul weather with very low cloud. There was no alternative but to return to base.

It was a bitter disappointment to the crew of the Lysander, but the necessary messages were sent out by the BBC in their 'Messages to France' programme. The reception near Poitiers was instructed to expect an aircraft on the following night when a second attempt would be made. The Lysander which had been converted to carry the GEE set was discarded and exchanged for another aircraft and Squadron Leader Wagland went along on the second trip to help with the map reading and give the aircraft the maximum assistance. Weather conditions had not shown a great deal of improvement, and the Moon Men would be put to the test.

Over the Continent, the weather forecast predicted good conditions, but there was a possibility of fog forming over Southern England during the night. Wing Commander Hodges decided to take off as early as possible, bearing in mind the state of the moon which was almost full at that time. It was their hope to be back in England close to midnight and beat the fog. The time for the round flight would be four hours and forty-five minutes, all being well.

Taking off from Tempsford on the same night, but one hour later than the Lysander on 'Operation Scenery II' were two other Lysanders, both on 'Operation Diable', and piloted by Flight Lieutenant Hankey and Flying Officer McBride.

The 'Scenery' Lysander took off at 20.45 hours and all went well. Without the GEE set to complicate matters, the gremlins behaved themselves and they crossed the French coastline with the usual amount of flak acknowledging their arrival. The flak was some distance from their flight path and caused them little concern. The Loire was crossed near Saumur and course was set south to Poitiers. The landing field was further to the south. Between Poitiers and Augouleme they were able to find a small town which had been selected as the last geographical pinpoint from which they could set a course on a timed approach to the position of the field.

The met forecast from England proved correct so far and the night was perfect with excellent visibility and a bright moon. Beneath them, all seemed quiet on the ground. They set off on their run to the target area and, at the appointed time, the downward identification light flashed out the morse signal letters. There was no response. In the full brightness of the moon, details of the ground were very clear and they could see individual fields clearly outlined.

Confident that they were over the target and landing area, the Lysander circled as they scanned the moonlit roads for a sign of movement. Before long, the headlights of a car could be seen approaching down the road beneath the aircraft. They watched the car carefully and saw it suddenly turn off into a field. In the headlights of the car, people were seen running in all directions.

A few seconds later the recognition signals flashed and the landing torches were switched on. The Lysander was circling at 200 feet and they quickly prepared to land. Within a matter of minutes, the aircraft was on the ground and running on a good, smooth stubble field. They turned and taxied back to No 1 torch before turning again into wind. Squadron Leader Wagland announced over the intercom that Robin Hooper was aboard, plus one other passenger, and they were airborne again in a minute or so. Everything had gone like clockwork, conditions created by the full moon had been ideal, and it transpired later that they had not been expected so early. This explained the last minute arrival of the ground party.

The early arrival of the Lysander had been an inconvenience, but it was to save their lives.

The return flight to Tangmere occasioned no trouble as they flew over France. Approaching the English coastline, a bank of low cloud could be seen ahead. Aerodrome control at Tangmere advised them over the radio that visibility was deteriorating and the present cloud base was down to 500 feet. It was the beginning of the longest night.

Flying high over Tangmere, it seemed inconceivable to Lewis Hodges and his navigator that the weather had clamped down underneath them. They were flying in bright moonlight, the horizon was clear and visibility perfect. Reports from below indicated that they were in for a tricky landing.

Tangmere came through again to advise that they would bring the aircraft down through the cloud for a ZZ landing. This was the instrument approach system at the time for airfields not equipped with Standard Beam Approach (SBA). As it happened, Standard Beam Approach would not have helped them. Their Lysander was not equipped with a set to receive SBA. The cloud top was approximately 1,500 feet, and the base had been reported at 500 feet. There would be at least 1,000 feet of blind flying on instruments. They were directed by the controller on the outbound heading and eventually they turned towards the direction of the runway for landing at a safe five miles from the airfield.

The aircraft entered cloud, descending on instruments only and maintaining a rate of descent and height as directed. They remained enveloped in cloud with the altimeter now reading 300 feet. At this height, they broke cloud base, and the very welcome runway lights were seen immediately ahead. The lights were shrouded in mist but their angle of approach could still be judged fairly accurately, and they were able to carry out a visual landing. The decision to leave early for the operation was singularly fortunate and they were all highly elated to have pulled off the rescue. As they taxied towards the control tower, the fog rolled in.

Wing Commander Hodges had already completed one night's work. His concern now was for the two other Lysanders still in the air. He proceeded immediately to the control tower to check. Both aircraft were already in touch by RT with the control tower on their return flight over the channel. Visibility was deteriorating as every minute passed and a thick fog was settling on the airfield, obscuring the runway. Met reports indicated similar conditions all over the South of England and the nearest diversion with any hope of improvement was at Woodbridge in Suffolk. The incoming Lysanders were short of the fuel necessary to carry out this diversion. The pilots had no alternative. An attempt at landing at Tangmere, or in the area of Tangmere, was the only solution, and time was running out.

Under normal circumstances, in the situation which now presented itself, Wing Commander Hodges would have had no hesitation in ordering the pilots to bale out. Such a decision was impossible. His pilots had agents aboard – agents they had picked up in France – and none had a parachute. Both aircraft would have to attempt a landing, albeit in conditions of atrocious visibility.

Both aircraft were due overhead at Tangmere about the same time. Wing Commander Hodges decided to take one of the aircraft at Tangmere, the Lysander piloted by McBride, and the other piloted by Hankey, he diverted to Ford, the neighbouring Naval airfield. He waited in the control tower to render any assistance or advice he could to the controller. McBride was 'talked down', as he himself had been, on to a ZZ approach and landing.

By this time visibility was down to 50 yards on the ground and conditions were extremely difficult. McBride was brought down and turned to the final approach entirely on instruments. The cloud bank was lowering and this was complicated by the ground fog. The aircraft made a first class approach and was on a very good heading for the runway. Over the end of the runway McBride was issued with the instruction to land straight ahead.

At this point McBride noticed the red light on top of the runway controller's caravan and he mistook it for hangar obstruction lights. Tense, taut and unsure, he called out on his RT 'You are flying me into the hangars!' and he opened up to go round again. He was assured by the controller that he had been on the correct flight path for a landing, and had been, in fact, directly over the runway. He remained in good RT contact with the control tower and came in once more on the final approach with everything set for a successful landing. While still in contact with the control tower on the approach the RT suddenly went dead. Nothing more was heard from McBride and Lewis Hodges realised immediately that he must have crashed on his final approach to the airfield.

By this time the fog was rolling in, thick, and impossible. It was clear that the rescue workers would have their work cut out to find McBride's aircraft. The most practical way to find the crash would be to go to the end of the runway and work back across the fields and ditches along the aircraft's final approach path. This was done. The searchers battled their way across fields and ditches for the best part of a mile. Conditions underfoot made it impossible to hurry. McBride's aircraft was found on the approach to the airfield. The Lysander stood on its nose, burning fiercely.

It was clear that he had no chance and he perished in the cockpit. Miraculously, the two French agents in the rear had escaped unhurt. Although considerably shaken, they were none the worse for their traumatic experience. Transport from the station had now arrived and both agents were returned to the cottage at Tangmere, the name given to the building where every agent remained until screened by the authorities. In a private funeral, Flying Officer McBride was buried on 20th December at Portfield Cemetery, Chichester.

Flight Lieutenant Hankey was in difficulties. He attempted to land at Ford to which he had been diverted, lost control in cloud, and crashed. Hankey and both French agents were killed. It had been a sad month for the Lysanders from Tempsford. On 10th December Flying Officer Bathgate had taken off in a Lysander with Flying Officer McBride on a double operation, code named 'Sten'. Weather conditions gradually deteriorated after take-off and visual fixes became increasingly impossible. McBride finally abandoned the operation and returned to base. After becoming airborne, Bathgate had made no contact with McBride or base, and nothing was ever seen or heard of Flying Officer Bathgate again.

The night of the 16th/17th was less disastrous for the Halifaxes.

In operation 'Wheelwright' three Halifaxes were involved. Halifax LL 120 left Tempsford at 21.15 hours with Warrant Officer Caldwell at the controls. His crew consisted of seven others and their mascot, a fox terrier puppy, was on board. After take-off, visibility was passable and they were able to navigate and map read until they were within approximately forty miles from their target area. The weather conditions then began to deteriorate but they pressed on relying entirely on their instruments. When they estimated their position to be over the target area, they circled for some time, hoping to pick up a pinpoint. Underneath, the cloud cover was extensive and thick and it was impossible for them to recognise their target. It was decided to retain the supplies which they carried on board, but to drop the leaflets regardless and this was done in the Angouleme area. Course was then set for home, with the conditions so impossible now that they had little to fear from either searchlights or fighters. Their base was shrouded in the same impossible conditions they had found over their target and a diversion was made to Woodbridge. Over Woodbridge, the weather-man had not relented and a landing through cloud in blind darkness was considered to be out of the question. A hurried discussion followed and it was decided to head for the Spilsby area, bale out, and trim the aircraft on a heading for the open sea. The decision to bale out over the flat fields around Spilsby in Lincolnshire was to prove their salvation.

Warrant Officer Caldwell called out to his crew behind him, 'Don't forget the pup!'

Without wasting any more precious time, his crew began to bale out, the first out carrying the small fox terrier puppy tucked under his left arm to allow his right arm freedom of movement to pull on the rip cord of the parachute. As they baled out, the pilot undid his straps anxiously waiting to see his navigator disappear, check that the aircraft was trimmed to clear the land over their estimated area, and left the Halifax to its own fate. The only mishap to the entire crew and their precious mascot on landing, was a broken ankle suffered by Flight Sergeant Morris. The darkness of the night was Stygian, with cloud base on the ground. The aircraft was reported later to have crashed into the sea by the Observer Corps. The time was 05.35.

Halifax DK 206 was piloted by Flight Lieutenant Gray with a crew of five plus two 'passengers'. They took off at 20.37 hours and ran into the same trouble as Warrant Officer Caldwell. The weather, after a few hours in the air, became impossible for further flying and they decided to return to base. Base was no better and,

RAF personnel at Tempsford, June 1942.

The equipment barn and cottages at Tempsford. The outer wooden cladding lent the brick-walled barn an innocent appearance.

(Left) Air Chief Marshal Sir Basil Embry.

(Centre) Farewell Ventura!

(Bottom) Mosquito B35 TA 634, re-coded EG-F in Pickard's memory, on show at Salisbury Hall.

like Warrant Officer Caldwell, they decided to divert to Woodbridge. They circled for an agonising length of time, hoping for a let-up in the weather. None came, and with fuel dwindling, Flight Lieutenant Gray called out to the crew to tighten their straps and stand by for a crash landing. The aircraft crash landed at Woodbridge at 05.05 hours, having spent almost nine hours in the air. The toll of killed and injured among the crew was complete. Flight Lieutenant Gray, Flying Officer Thomas and Flight Sergeant Fry were killed. Pilot Officer Shine, Flying Officer Craven and Sergeant Betts received serious injuries. By the strangest quirk of fate, neither of their two 'passengers' received a scratch and both were able to proceed to London the same day.

Halifax LK 899 left on Operation Wheelwright from Tempsford four minutes before DK 206, at 20.34 hours. Piloted by Flying Officer Harborow and carrying a crew of six others, the aircraft set course for France. The weather over France had begun to close in and, by the time they had reached their target area, they could not identity any definite position. Like the others, Flying Officer Harborow spent some time in the area hoping that the weather might improve. There was no joy and sadly they returned to base, gripped and griping about their journey being unnecessary. However poor the conditions in France, they were exceeded over England and Tempsford was non-existent. Diverting to Woodbridge in the hope that they would have better luck with the weather, a lower altitude, and the possibility of the ground mist being cleared by the sea breezes, they began to lose height in the direction of Woodbridge. For some time they circled at a height of less than 500 feet, hoping for a break in the cloud to indicate their proximity to Woodbridge Airfield. The weather continued to be appalling with visibility nil, and Flying Officer Harborow was conscious of his fuel running low.

The flaps were lowered to reduce speed and the aircraft continued to lose height as all eyes peered out into the ominous gloom. Before they were able to see anything and take avoiding action, the aircraft struck a pylon which spun the aircraft round, the last of their height was lost but, by good fortune, they were able to crash land on a mud bank off Bawdsey which absorbed most of the shock. In the complete darkness, every escape hatch was opened and the crew piled out with most of them receiving only shock and minor injuries. Each moved individually away from the sound of the sea towards dry land. Once back on terra firma, heads were counted and Flying Officer McMaster was missing. With local help a search party was mounted next morning as soon as there was light enough. By this time the sea had rolled in over the mud bank. McMaster was found, drowned. He had apparently been knocked unconscious and in the confusion of hitting the pylon and ditching immediately after, his absence had not been noticed until it was too late.

For RAF Tempsford, it had been a long night. It was not difficult to count the cost. Of the three Halifaxes and three Lysanders which went out, one solitary Lysander remained intact upon return, beating the weather by the skin of its teeth. The cost in experienced aircrew was equally disastrous, lost within a hairsbreadth of home There was little joy over Christmas in December of 1943 at Tempsford.

The operations report for the month of December is a record of sadness.

> Adverse weather conditions prevailed during this month and only a very small number of operations could be carried out and these achieved only a small measure of success. The squadron were most unfortunate too in regard to casualties and the night of the 16th/17th December when the weather unexpectedly closed down, resulted in one of the most tragic pages of the unit's history. Three Halifaxes and three Lysanders were out on this night and of the former two crash landed, Flight Lieutenant Gray and two of his crew being killed and the remainder badly injured. Flying Officer Harborow met with better luck, all the crew escaping with the exception of Flying Officer McMaster who had apparently been struck unconscious and was eventually found drowned. Of the third Halifax, decision was made by the Captain – Warrant Officer Caldwell – to bale out and all made it successfully, only Flight Sergeant Morris receiving foot injury.
>
> Wing Commander Hodges, Flight Lieutenant Hankey and Flying Officer McBride were piloting the Lysanders and in each case the pick ups were carried out successfully. Wing Commander Hodges fortunately was out earlier and returned before conditions were at the worst and was just able to make a very

difficult landing – this was the only bright spot of the night as Flight Lieutenant Hooper was his return passenger. The other two pilots had completed their jobs successfully but on returning to base found conditions almost hopeless, no diversion possible and owing to their having passengers with them they could not bale out. Blind landings had to be attempted and in each case aircraft ran into the ground and the pilots were killed. This was not the only loss suffered by the Lysander flight as on the 10th Flying Officer Bathgate failed to return from operations, no news whatsoever being available about him.

Fourteen sorties were carried out by the Halifax flight comprising 23 operations and of these nine were successful, failure of the others was largely attributable to the weather conditions.

Seven sorties only were undertaken by the Lysanders and two of these were carried out by Wing Commander Hodges, who on his second attempt was able to bring back Flight Lieutenant Hooper, three met with disaster and the other two were not successful. Experiments were made in adapting GEE to these aircraft, but so far it is impossible to state whether it will prove a success.

CHAPTER SEVEN

L'Affaire Déricourt

As early as 7th August 1940, the main headquarters of the Germans in Paris received complaints of sabotage activities by the French. Although France had fallen and the Battle of Britain lay ahead, there were countless Frenchmen who refused to accept the presence of the German soldiers on French soil, and many willingly gave their lives in attempts to hinder and throw the proverbial spanner in the works of the massive German war machine.

The results at first were pathetically small for the supreme price they had to pay. There was a sad lack of unified direction, correlation of effort, and the wherewithal to make both work. To this end, Special Operations Executive had been formed in Britain.

It is not within the compass of Charles Pickard's story to deal with the birth, growth and expansion of SOE at length. Suffice it to say that the organisation suffered growing pains, mistakes were made as in all spheres of war, but expand and succeed it did. By the tail end of 1942 when Pick took over No 161 Squadron at Tempsford in October, SOE had become a viable and thriving unit. The agents had to be screened, hand-picked, resolute and tough. As Hugh Dalton had suggested, they were of varying nationalities. They varied from the gentle and lovely Noor Inayat Khan, through a young chartered accountant in England not yet fully qualified in his profession, to the toughest in France who had already received their baptism of fire.

After Charles Pickard had taken over 161 Squadron, Henri Déricourt was posted to Tempsford. As his name suggests. Déricourt was born in France, of French parents on 2nd September 1909. He had made his career as a more than competent civil pilot and had the very considerable number of close on 4,000 flying hours to his credit before he joined SOE. He was said to have earned £300 a week prior to the war as a trick aerobat. He was a man of keen and

L'Affaire Déricourt

swift intelligence which he combined with an uncommonly steady nerve. With a witty turn of speech and a persuasive manner, he had a flashy taste in clothes. He was well known and not disliked in such society as international pilots would frequent. Before the war, Déricourt did a little courier work for at least one continental secret service, but nothing to do with Britain until he joined SOE.

In 1939/1940, Henri Déricourt served in the French Air Force as a transport and test pilot before going back to civil flying. He was in Aleppo when it was overrun by the Allies in July 1941, and, with several other pilots, he was offered work with Imperial Airways, the predecessor of BOAC. Déricourt said that he would like to accept the offer but had to revisit France on private business first. He returned to France, married, and gave his wife a large sum in cash. Having resettled his family near Paris. Déricourt was ready to escape to England.

His contacts were not found wanting and in August of 1942 he reached Glasgow from Gibraltar along an escape line via Marseilles. He was greeted by a Free French staff officer on the platform of Euston Station two days later. However, he had already made up his mind not to work for the Gaullists. He was promptly taken up by 'F' Section, the main British body organising French subversion, although the security authorities reported that they could not give him a clean bill. His journey from Syria to England through occupied France might well have exposed him to pressure to become a German agent. However, the HQ staff of 'F' Section were delighted to see him, with one exception – and this exception later became one of his strongest supporters. They determined to use him as Air Movements Officer in northern France. He was given parachute training and a short spell on Lysanders during which he made the acquaintance and later the friendship of both Dorothy and Charles Pickard.

On 22nd/23rd January of 1943, Déricourt made his first jump into France not far from Orleans. With all haste he set course for Paris where he rejoined his wife and lived quite openly under his own name in his own flat. He had wit enough to maintain that he was too well known to do anything else. He was very fond of his wife and she was not the sort of woman who would be any good at concealing her identity. His Paris friends thought that he had spent the last five months in Marseilles. His Marseilles friends, whom he occasionally visited in the course of his work, thought he had spent them in Paris. He did not enlighten either.

Déricourt had been selected as Air Movements Officer to SOE and the various networks in France because of his considerable flying experience. Suitable fields for landing in a short space had to be selected, wind speeds had to be judged and the small, almost primitive but effective flare path consisting of three hand torches had to be laid out at the last moment. The work seemed to be hand tailored for Déricourt as his pilot experience gave him a sound schooling in the requirements and hazards of landing an aircraft in a small area in the middle of the night. His first operation was arranged through the wireless operators attached to the Prosper network. It took place near Poitiers on 17th/18th March, 1943. Two Lysanders were involved with four agents and returned to England with another four. The flight was successful. On 14th/15th April he organised another double Lysander operation in the Loire water-meadows under the walls of Amboise. Four more agents arrived and one left.

Of the four who arrived, one by the name of Frager accompanied Déricourt downstream to Tours where the mother-in-law of one of the other agents in Frager's flight to France, Dubois, was the school's headmistress. Inconveniently the Gestapo called the following morning while Frager was at breakfast and Frager, warned just in time, was able to make good his escape. His first impressions of Monsieur Déricourt were unsavoury. In fact, the Gestapo visit was purely a routine one to check up on the school's text books and library. But Frager had his doubts and it gave him a poor opening impression of Déricourt. The following night Déricourt received another Lysander midway between Le Mans and Tours. The futures of these two agents in the latest Lysander did not concern him. Julienne Aisner was returned to England to be trained as his potential courier. In the last Lysander which arrived while he was on this tour on 22nd/23rd April, he returned to England himself on instructions from London. His 'welcome home' present to Dorothy Pickard was a bottle of exquisite French perfume.

After drinks and dinner at the home of Dorothy and Pick, the trio sat round the fire to discuss the war in general, France in particular, but never a word about the work in which Déricourt was involved. Pick drew on his much loved and inevitable pipe. It was a quiet domestic scene. Young Nick Pickard was now four months old and safely asleep in his cot in one of the bedrooms. Ming however was not lying in her customary position at Pick's feet in front of the fire. It was some time before her absence was noticed by the Pickards. Dorothy rose to find the dog in case for some reason she had been locked outside.

Ming had taken herself off quietly and unobtrusively earlier in the evening and now lay at full length in front of baby Nick Pickard's cot. No amount of coaxing on the part of Dorothy would induce Ming to return to the sitting room while Déricourt was there. She was happy to look seriously at Dorothy as she spoke to her, wag her tail, but refused to budge. When their guest had been seen to the door and had left, Dorothy mentioned Ming's strange behaviour to Pick, suggesting in the hallway that Ming might be ill. Together they went straight to Nick's bedroom but the dog had gone. They returned to the sitting room wondering at the ways of canines. Ming lay stretched out on the carpet in front of the fire.

Flights from Tempsford continued with increasing frequency as the weather improved into springtime and summer. In May of 1943, Charles Pickard was promoted to Group Captain to take over Lissett with Squadron Leader Lewis (Bob) Hodges promoted to Wing Commander taking command of 161 Squadron at Tempsford. Flying Officer J. A. Broadley who had been Pickard's navigator throughout their extensive operational career together was awarded the DFC in addition to his DFM in April of 1943, while at Tempsford.

Déricourt remained in England for a few days' staff discussions before parachuting blind into the Gatinais region of France during a 'dark' period on the night of 5th/6th May. His next operation, on the night of 13th/14th May involved two Lysanders from a ground in the Cher Valley, a few miles east of Tours. Four agents arrived safely and one was returned to England. The Prosper network was being strengthened by these agents who had been sent out to re-form the 'Inventor' circuit working alongside 'Donkeyman'.

A month was to pass before Déricourt organised his next operation, also a double Lysander job. On the night of 16th/17th

June the two Lysanders landed on a clear moonlit night in the Loire Valley seven miles north-east of Angers, close to the Loire's junction with the Sarthe. Three doomed women climbed down the steps from the Lysanders. Cecily Lefort (Alice) who was to act as courier to the 'Jockey' network; Diana Rowden (Paulette), courier to Acrobat, and Noor Inayat Khan (Madeleine), wireless operator to Cinema which was a sub-circuit of Prosper.

A week later Déricourt was back on the Amboise ground receiving a Lysander flown by Squadron Leader Hugh Verity. Two agents were delivered and one left, accompanied by an escaping airman. The night was 23rd/24th June, the night of the long knives which spelled disaster to the Prosper network.

The first operation by Déricourt after his return from England took place on 13th/14th May. The agent who returned to London by Lysander from the Cher Valley was Major Francis Alfred Suttill. Major Suttill was the son of an Englishman, born in Manchester, who had settled in Lille and married a Frenchwoman.

In October of 1942, Francis Suttill was parachuted into France to take over the direction of the Prosper network. The network continued to bear his code name and covered Paris itself extending down the whole of the Loire Valley. It was the largest and most important of the 'French Section' networks in France to which a number of others had allowed themselves to become, in varying degrees, tributary. Of 'Prosper', Lieutenant Colonel Buckmaster writes in *Specially Employed* that it comprised some 10,000 people.

The agent taken back to England on the double Lysander flight on the night of 13th/14th May out of the Cher Valley, east of Tours, was Prosper himself – Major Francis Alfred Suttill. He returned to France shortly after to re-join the Prosper network, the landing in France being organised by Henri Déricourt. Suttill's second in command was known to the network by the name of Archambault.

From January 1941 until April 1942 he was attached as Liaison Officer to the Polish Army in the Middle East. He was then transferred to SOE 'French Section' for training as a wireless operator and was first parachuted into France in the Touraine district to take up duties as wireless operator and second-in-command to 'Prosper'. He held the rank of Major, and landed in France on the 1st November, 1942.

Between two trips to England, Déricourt conducted a grand total of seventeen operations involving twenty-one aircraft. Forty-three people had entered France and sixty-seven had left under his care. He was later to magnify this figure to 240 people.

It is almost impossible to ascertain the exact time when Monsieur Henri Déricourt became involved with SS Sturmbannführer Hans Kieffer and SS Sturmbannführer Karl Boemelburg at 84 Avenue Foch. It will be remembered that the security authorities in London could not give him a clean bill in September of 1942 on his first arrival in London via Gibraltar and Glasgow 'because his journey from Syria to England through occupied France might well have exposed him to pressure to become a German agent'. He was later to suggest to Jean Overton Fuller, as she relates in *Double Webs*, that the few days of staff discussion in London between 23rd April and 6th May had some bearing on the subject. He had, he said, been approached by 'another organisation in London', not the French Section and by implication not SOE, to approach the Germans on his return to France. Nothing got on the public record to bear this out. He had, in fact been summoned to London to receive a reprimand from Squadron Leader Verity for having endangered a Lysander through an ill-placed flare path.

It is certain that Déricourt, alias 'Gilbert' to the underground, was well known at 84 Avenue Foch, headquarters of the Gestapo in Paris. Photostat copies of the mail being sent to England through 'Gilbert' were filed for future reference at 84 Avenue Foch.

Déricourt arrived back in France from England on the night of 23rd/24th June, 1943. On 24th June Prosper, Archambault and their collaborators were arrested. A German, Ernest, who was on Kieffer's staff as chief interrogator of all the major agents of the British SOE, French Section, survived the war. After the war he was examined and released. On the subject of Déricourt he was in a position to be quite explicit.

The report made by Ernest is an appalling indictment against someone who had been attached to Pickard's squadron and was later promoted to Air Movements Officer for SOE in France. If Cole had established a precedent for treachery, Henri Déricourt was running him a close second. The following is part of Ernest's report as given in *Double Webs (Putnam & Co Ltd, 1958)*.

Up to the end of 1943, Gilbert was the agent of Boemelburg, Chief of the Gestapo in France, and came directly under him. At the time of the departure of Boemelburg for Vichy, towards the end of 1943 or early in 1944, he became the agent of Kieffer and worked immediately under him . . .

We came to know of Gilbert's landing ground near Angers and Kieffer was, from time to time, aware of BBC messages which gave warning of forthcoming landings. Gilbert passed on to Kieffer some of the mail and information about the arrival of aircraft. In return, he obtained a promise that the Germans would never shoot down or capture any of the aircraft landing on his landing grounds. Thus he could receive or despatch aircraft with a perfectly easy mind. The British agents' mail for London, which 'Gilbert' passed on to Kieffer, was photographed by our service and then returned to 'Gilbert' who sent it on to London. I do not suppose that he passed over the entire mail to Kieffer.

'Prosper', 'Archambault' and their collaborators were arrested as a result of reports, intended for London, which 'Gilbert' had passed over to Boemelburg. After their arrest, Kieffer handed to me photographic copies of the reports that Prosper and Archambault had sent to London.

The copies contained almost complete information about their activities, together with addresses and names. It was these reports which enabled us to bring off our great round-up of the 'Prosper' organisation.

The question still remains unresolved. At what time did Henri Déricourt make contact with 84 Avenue Foch? He became attached to 161 Squadron under Charles Pickard towards the end of 1942. Contrary to the recommendations of British Security, he was appointed Air Movements Officer to SOE in January of 1943. That he was a man of courage there is no doubt. To walk the tightrope as a double agent requires more than a nimble imagination backed by the powers of persuasion. Of these Déricourt was well endowed. If, by his own admission, he did not become involved in 84 Avenue Foch until the suggestion was made to him in London between the 23rd April and 5th/6th May, 1943, one question remains to be answered. Why did Pickard report on 25th February, 1943:

L'Affaire Déricourt

A very striking note in this operation was the fact of remaining unmolested by any Germans, as the fact of first making so many circuits before landing must have caused some attention.

Archambault, alias Gilbert Norman, the accountant under training in London, was shot at Mauthausen Extermination Camp on 6th September 1944. Prosper, alias Major Francis Alfred Suttill, was eliminated and his execution was presumed.

Fifteen of the fifty women agents who had been sent from England to France fell into German hands. Only three of these fifteen survived. The Germans divided these captives into two groups, seven going into Karlsruhe Civil Prison in the Rhine Valley while the other eight went into the concentration camp at Ravensbruck, fifty miles north of Berlin. They had never been tried, but they were sharing cells with convicts, except for Noor Inayat Khan, the first of them to arrive who was long kept in chains in a cell by herself in the subsidiary prison of Pforzheim. There they might have stayed until the war was over, had not an officious wardress been moved by the idea that the position of these women was somewhat irregular.

One morning in July 1944, Vera Leigh, Diana Rowden, Andrée Borrel and Sonia Olschanesky were suddenly taken by train to the concentration camp at Natzwiler in Alsace. In the late evening all the prisoners in the camp were ordered into their huts. The four new arrivals were taken to the camp crematorium and each was given a lethal injection. The other four at Karlsruhe – Noor Inayat Khan, Yolande Beekman, Eliane Plewman and Madeleine Damerment – knew nothing of their companions' fate. No more did the last three know of Noor Inayat Khan's presence nearby until she joined them on 11th September. Orders for them also had now come down over Kaltenbrunner's signature and they were warned the same evening to be ready to move next day. The following day they were moved by car and train until they reached a station not far from Munich at midnight. They were made to walk uphill together to a strange camp. It was Dachau.

They were put into separate cells overnight to be awakened at first light in the morning. Together they were called out into a sandy yard, and told to kneel down by a wall. They saw blood stains in the sand and knew their fate. They knelt down, two and two, each pair holding hands. An SS man came up behind them and shot each of them neatly through the back of the neck.

Of the eight who had been sent to Ravensbruck the work parties proved too much for Cecily Lefort and her health finally broke down early in 1945. She allowed herself to be put on a transport to the Jugendlager, a nominal rest camp, where sick prisoners were sent to waste away from starvation or the merciful end was expedited more promptly in the gas chamber. At about the same time Madame Rudellat vanished and it was presumed that she had gone the same way. Eileen Nearne made a break from a work party in mid-April and, by a remarkable feat of bravery and level-headedness picked her way across ruined Germany to succeed in meeting up with the Americans. Yvonne Baseden also succeeded in getting away from Ravensbruck. She fell ill with tuberculosis in February and, with the help of another inmate, she managed to escape from a work party and was helped into Sweden by a Red Cross team.

Three others of the young agents were less fortunate. Violette Szabo, Denise Bloch and Lilian Rolfe were sent out together on a working party and found the work endurable. On completion of their stint in the first work party, they asked to go on another. Their second group turned out to be much more fierce and by early February only the irrepressible cheerfulness and stamina of Violette Szabo could help to keep the other two going. The three were not dying quickly enough. A few days later, on an order from Berlin, they were taken out and shot together just as the four girls had been shot at Dachau.

Odette Sansom was accorded special treatment at Ravensbruck. Mistakenly, but fortunately, some Germans thought that she was Winston Churchill's niece by marriage and she owed her survival to the resultant confusion. She was kept for many months on end in solitary confinement in a small, dark concrete cell, subjected to extremes of heat and cold, light and darkness, close by the execution ground where every day she could hear the shots disposing of her friends and allies. Towards the bitter end it became clear to the camp commandant, Fritz Suhren, that the much vaunted 'thousand year Reich' was beginning to show definite signs of chinks in its armour and the decay was being hastened by the march of the Allies on Berlin. Fritz made his own plans. He would take Odette Sansom in a smart sports car, drive her into the American lines in the hope that her influence would save his own neck. He misjudged the temper of Odette Sansom and the generosity of the Americans.

Belsen was freed by the British forces on 15th April 1945. Many will remember the indescribable film of the camp which was taken at the time of its liberation. So many millions in the free world could not believe nor comprehend the extent of the Nazi atrocities and the film, with few comments, showed the inmates of Belsen lying in heaps or walking around without showing the slightest sign of emotion or recognition in the last stages of emaciation. The film was called *Proof Positive*.

Unnoticed among the hundreds of prisoners suffering from the ravages of a typhus epidemic and prevailing dysentry a Frenchwoman was suffering from both. She called herself Madame Gauthier and had arrived at Belsen from another camp six weeks before. When she arrived she was then as well as anyone could be amid the prevailing lack of food, fuel, clothing, decency and privacy. She was not long in Belsen before she fell dangerously ill. When the camp was captured, she was too far gone with disease, or too steeped and brainwashed in her cover story, or both, to mention to a soul who or what she had been. Unnoticed to the last, she died on St George's Day or the day after, and her body was huddled with twenty thousand others into one of the huge mass graves. Her name was Yvonne Rudellat.

The betrayal and fall of the Prosper network on the night of 23rd/24th June, 1943, was a severe blow to the underground in France. The broken pieces were destined eventually to be picked up, along with the 'Farmer' circuit into a new circuit called 'Spiritualist' by Rene Dumont-Guillemet, who made his first trip to England by Lysander on the night of 16th/17th October. The trip was organised by Déricourt from his Amboise ground.

Four days later, Déricourt was at work again, on his Hudson ground north of Angers. Four arrived and four left. Of the latter, one was important – Frager, who was running his own network assisted by Roger Bardet who was his trusted second-in-command. Frager had been suspicious of Déricourt ever since his first operation when he just managed to escape the Germans at the school. He was even more suspicious now and he was going to London expressly to report his conviction that Déricourt was a German agent. The pilots and aircrews from Tempsford, at risk of life and limb, were certainly carrying an odd collection of agents, double agents and a wrangle of mischief unknown to them.

When Frager arrived at Angers with his friend and second-in-command for the flight to England, Déricourt was intensely annoyed. He advised Frager, truly enough, that it ran against the rules of all security and common sense to bring along a friend to see one off. Both Roger Bardet and Frager maintained an air of mystery when then met. A sharp quarrel broke out over dinner near Angers and was continued at the landing ground. Frager wanted to know whether Déricourt had read the reports which were being flown to England in the Lysanders and, if so, why? The acrid discussion followed and increased even as Frager entered the Hudson. It ended at the door of the Hudson with Frager closing his hand on the butt of the revolver in his pocket. Déricourt changed his tune and asked half plaintively.

'Why do you mistrust me, Paul?'

The aircraft took off and Déricourt's question went unanswered.

Frager crossed to England in the Hudson with the declared 'primary object' of arraigning Déricourt as a traitor. He reported that a mysterious 'Colonel Heinrich', who was in fact Sergeant Bleicher of the Abwehr, had stated definitely that Gilbert was working for the Germans. It is not clear why Bleicher let out this important piece of information. He mentioned it early in August during a chat with Roger Bardet and Frager over a glass of beer. Frager had made the flight to England on the 20th/21st October to denounce Déricourt. No action was taken and the charges were put down to Frager's undoubted excitability. However, the charges were being re-inforced from other quarters. One of Déricourt's opposite numbers in the same section, George Pichard (Oyster), was reported to have good reason to believe that a 'Frenchman holding a commission in the British Army, in charge of air operations in the Paris and Angers districts had betrayed to the Germans two men and a woman who were landed sometime in August and were picked up by the Gestapo very shortly after their arrival'. The possibility that Déricourt was on the wrong side was now considered a matter of extreme secrecy and urgency. It is a sad reflection that Henri

L'Affaire Déricourt

Déricourt, whether guilty or not, received an instruction to return to London only on 4th February, 1944. It was decided on the 21st February that Déricourt should not be allowed to return to France.

Déricourt's training made him unable to overlook the lack of direct proof of guilt and helped him to see how flimsy much of the circumstantial evidence was. The British Security Service offered a more direct and hostile opinion.

'Although it is only fair to say that 'Gilbert' makes a good personal impression under interrogation, and that his antecedents seem to be unexceptionable, we should, if the decision were entirely ours, regard the case against him as serious enough to prevent him undertaking any further intelligence work outside this country. In view of the facts indeed we feel that this is the recommendation which we must make.'

The feelings of Major Henri Frager (Paul), at long last, seemed to be vindicated. It is sad to report that these feelings did not extend to his own friend and second-in-command, Roger Bardet. Roger Bardet was a Frenchman who was trusted implicitly by Frager in Frager's own network. When Frager stood at the door of the Hudson remonstrating with Déricourt and drew the vicious argument to a close by placing his hand on the butt of his revolver, he made two mistakes. Bardet was standing beside Déricourt on the landing ground. The mistakes made by Frager cost him his life. The gun should have been pointed at Bardet and Frager should have pulled the trigger.

Bardet had informed Bleicher of the Abwehr over a long period of time on the entire workings of the Frager network. In consequence of this betrayal to Bleicher by Bardet, Major Frager was hanged at Buchenwald on 4th October, 1944.

Déricourt, the man who had joined Pickard's squadron and whom Pick had befriended in 1942/1943, was not finished with Britain yet. He was restricted to an hotel in London to complete questioning. There are, as we know, worse places than an hotel in Piccadilly to be 'restricted'. The questioning arrangement went on until the end of August 1944. On 1st September he was freed, to rejoin the Royal Air Force, in a flying capacity.

September of that year had been momentous and disastrous for the agents, men and women, who had been caught. Déricourt took to the air in a Spitfire. The story of his intrigue might never have been written after 9th September. He was shot down. There followed a period of eight months' hospitalisation during which he made satisfactory progress. On 8th May the war with Germany ended. Monsieur Déricourt was free to return to his home.

After a post-war career as colourful as his earlier exploits, Déricourt was eventually arrested by the French in Paris on the 26th November 1947. His trial did not take place until 7th June 1948. The French wanted his head badly. He obviously bore a charmed life. On intervention from London, Déricourt was set free. His 'arrangement' with 84 Avenue Foch that no British aircraft should be molested on landing or take-off in France, while delivering agents, may well have influenced the decision of the British authorities.

Oddly, his interrogation in London after which he was relieved of his duty as 'Air Movement Officer' in Northern France, took place in the same month as the raid against Amiens Prison was being planned. The number of underground workers awaiting liquidation by the Gestapo in Amiens Prison who were perhaps betrayed by the intrigue of Henri Déricourt, will never be known. The information received by 84 Avenue Foch from agent 'BOE 48' put prisoners into Amiens Prison. It would be left to agent 'BOE 48's friend and former Commanding Officer to get them out – Charles Pickard.

CHAPTER EIGHT

The Mosquito and the Wheelbarrow

> I turn green with envy when I see the Mosquito. The British knock together a beautiful wooden aircraft that every piano factory there is building ... There is nothing the British do not have.
>
> Reichmarshal Hermann Goering

Promotion to Group Captain in May and a posting to Lissett was not a pleasing prospect for Charles Pickard. Being removed from operational flying was bad enough. Insult was added to injury when he found that the mainstay of the aircraft at Lissett came, in his opinion, out of the pot with Pontius. He did not have a high regard for the Ventura bomber which was slow, ugly and unmanoeuverable. He was only too willing to agree with the other pilots who had already dubbed the Ventura 'the flying pig'. In company with Bostons and Mosquitos, the Ventura had been used in the attack on the Philips factory at Eindhoven in 1942, with losses in Venturas being greater than the other two aircraft combined. It had, recorded Group Captain Pickard, 'the flying characteristics of a suitcase and the elegance of a turnip.'

It was arranged that Dorothy should join Pick from Tempsford when he had time to settle down. Upon his arrival at Lissett and before the rot of boredom and frustration had set in, he telephoned Dorothy to ask her to make her way to the nearby town of Scarborough where he would meet her at the station. Dorothy duly trudged across country by train and arrived very tired and bedraggled in the middle of the night. The station was empty of patrons, and there was no sign of Pick. She telephoned Lissett to be advised that her husband was flying, but a driver would arrive shortly to take her to her hotel in Scarborough. Her mood was in keeping with the dreary outlook of a deserted station, blacked out, at night wartime.

The hotel was not much of an improvement on the railway station, apart from the lights. It was a gaunt building of doubtful vintage where the horses had obviously been removed in a hurry to accommodate the humans. With the horses had gone the heat.

'There's a war on!' was the inevitable excuse from bread-filled bangers to cold hotels for horses. Dorothy ordered a drink.

Wrapped in her beaver lamb coat, she awaited with impatience the arrival of Pick from night flying. Her thoughts of the utter dreariness, the cold and the unpleasantness of her surroundings quickly evaporated as Pick bounced into the room. His mood was no less antagonistic.

'I'm not staying on this bloody station. There's no operational flying and I've just had it! I'm going to get transferred, so don't bother looking for a house. You can go back to Tempsford in a couple of days. I've had more excitement chasing rabbits and washing nappies!'

Dorothy found her way back to Tempsford, and Pick began to badger for a posting. The tempo of the man was vested in a great and restless spirit. He won. The month of May was spent at Lissett in a rest period he did not enjoy. The month of June was spent trying to remedy the error of the ways of the Royal Air Force. By July he was posted to RAF Sculthorpe . . . and Mosquitos.

The name of de Havilland has been synonymous with aircraft for a very long time. Prior to his abiding and all-consuming interest in aircraft, Sir Geoffrey de Havilland was vying with Harry Ferguson to improve motor bikes. Having done so both went their separate ways, Harry Ferguson to produce one of the finest tractors in the world and Geoffrey de Havilland to concentrate his energies and attention in flying machines.

The grandfather of Sir Geoffrey de Havilland may not have recognised genius but he did recognise tenacity of purpose and the ability to get things done. He had set aside £1,000 to be left in his will to his grandson. He was also able to recognise a certain lack of funds for the development of the flying machine project. In the event he gave Geoffrey and his brother, who was equally involved in the scheme, the £1,000 which was their share of his will. Together they hired a shed on a farm with a piece of land adjoining which they considered suitable for their first assault into the air. The £1,000 proved of immense value at the time. The de Havilland brothers **were** able to make one machine, crash it shortly after take-off and rebuild the same machine with certain modifications all for the sum given to them by their grandfather. On the second attempt, their brain child was flown by Sir Geoffrey's brother. It managed to take off, make a circuit of the field, and land more or less in one piece. The de Havilland empire was on its way.

Throughout the years the firm expanded, backers who had the vision to appreciate the value of aircraft were not easy to find, and it may truly be said that the de Havilland contribution to the 1939/1945 war effort was second to none. It would be of more than academic interest to know how many pilots in the Royal Air Force and in the Empire Air Training Groups made their first prop swinging, cockpit drill, take off into wind, climbing and gliding turns, and finally landing this dream of a very sensitive aircraft known as the DH 82A, the inimitable de Havilland Tiger Moth, dating back to 1928 and still flying.

Neither Sir Geoffrey de Havilland nor his close-knit team of aerodynamic experts were content to rest on their laurels.

When war began, it was obvious that certain sectors of the manufacturing community in Britain would, at worst, be out of work and, at best, suffer from a recession in business. Chief among these was the furniture making industry. The industry had its uses, particularly when France was taken over by the Germans and non-existent airfields were scattered with non-operational aircraft made of wood to draw the attention of diligent eyes in an effort to attract valuable bomb loads on aircraft whose wings of plyboard were supported by wooden trestles. The Royal Air Force was not slow to reply and not without a sense of humour, so remarkably lacking in a German at war. Legend has it that with every known precaution a raid was mounted on these airfields. The squadrons would go in first to mark the target. The Germans rubbed their hands in absolute glee at the thought of precious bomb loads being dropped on their ersatz aircraft. Not one of the bomb loads exploded. 'Time fused' reasoned the Germans. An inspection of the bombs littering the airfield two days later accounted for the absence of bangs. The bombs, in their entirety, were made of wood.

The production of wooden bombs was hardly a full time job for the furniture making industry in general. The brains at the head of de Havilland put their heads together. Why allow the expertise of the timber industry go to waste? Once more the genius of the de Havilland headmasters came to light. It was suggested by someone who had a brighter idea than most, that an aircraft be constructed of wood. The idea at first sounded slightly more than ridiculous. It would catch fire easily. It would not stand up to the stresses and strains of speeds. In its favour it was pointed out that it would not rust in the rain. It was a revolutionary idea from the outset. In 1940/1941, Britain was looking for revolutionary ideas. From the heart of de Havilland the Wooden Wonder was born.

The Hurricane and the Spitfire in the Battle of Britain had fired the imagination and inspired undying affection of pilots and public alike. In the new and daring concept of an aircraft made almost entirely of wood, its extreme versatility was to outshine even its more humble and universally acclaimed Tiger Moth predecessor. A shetland pony plays many parts, but none on the race course. Stripped of any armour or armaments, the twin engined Mosquito relied entirely on its speed to evade the enemy. In this it was remarkably successful and on high flying, or low flying, photographic reconnaissance work it was without peer. Graceful and swift as a swallow it had the inherent characteristics and handling qualities of a viceless thoroughbred horse. Cast in this mould, it is small wonder that the Mosquito made a niche for itself in the immortals of British aviation, adding an impressive laurel to the outstanding work of the de Havilland Company, and so beloved by the pilots and navigators who had the privilege of flying them. The countless operational uses of the Mosquito would require a volume in itself. To see was to admire. To fly was to love.

Charles Pickard had kept in touch with de Havilland throughout his entire flying career. Although Sir Geoffrey was not aware of it, Pick's idea of heaven after a long and dangerous operation in a heavy bomber over enemy territory was the regular entry in his log book – 'DH 82A. Solo Aerobatics'.

In July of 1943, Charles Pickard was moved to take over the command of RAF Sculthorpe. On 1st August he had his first introduction to the Mosquito which had by now proved its worth – although made of wood! He flew with Squadron Leader Bowen in two separate flights of fifty minutes and one hour twenty-five. In just over two hours of familiarisation, Pick had mastered the complicated instrument panel, thrown the aircraft around to acquire the feel of it in different attitudes, and 'opened the taps' to maximum speed. His first impression of perfection in the Mosquito's handling characteristics were made by comparison. His previous two flights had been made in the old Ventura, flown by many and loved by none. Heavy, slow, cumbersome and with precious little ability to get out of its own road, the Ventura was about the most unpopular aircraft in the Royal Air Force. After coming straight off the Ventura, in which he made numerous flights, Pick was quick to recognise the thoroughbred blood of the Mosquito and its performance matched his temperament to perfection.

Throughout August and September Charles Pickard and Alan Broadley were able to team up again in Mosquitos, separated as they had been for a time when Pick was flying Lysanders to France. They piled up the hours with an average of three flights each day. Low level flights, formation flying, high and low level bombing, and a remarkable number of flights and landings on one engine. Of these, the flights and landings on one engine were to be put to the ultimate test on their first operational sortie in the Mosquito.

On 3rd October the holiday was over. Pick and Alan Broadley set off in Mosquito 'F' for Exeter to rendezvous with other Mosquitos for an attack against the Power Works at Pont Chateau. It was to be a quick in-and-out job as the Power Works were heavily defended and they hoped to rely on their speed to keep clear of enemy fighters on the way back. Bombed up at Exeter, the aircraft took off at 12.45, flying fast across the channel in close formation. The aircraft ran into no trouble until the approach and run-in to the target at Pont Chateau. As they approached the target, the anti-aircraft gunfire from the ground was both intense and accurate. The Mosquitos held to their course, dropped their bombs successfully, and made to turn and high tail it for home. Pick's Mosquito was hit by the withering fire on the starboard engine, caught fire, and seized up. His immediate reaction was to cut off the fuel to his engine. With the engine seized, he was unable to feather the prop fully and this caused additional drag and slowed down his speed, now entirely dependent on his port engine.

Reliance on the one engine caused him to change his return flight plan and they made for Predannock in the south of England. The dependability of the Mosquito was put to the acid test. On one engine they flew a total of 370 miles to land safely at Predannack. They were not alone. Five of the Mosquitos on this flight collected severe flak damage, yet all managed to return to England. On their first Mosquito operation, the aircraft had survived its baptism under fire, with Pick and Alan Broadley more than impressed. Nor was Pick forgetful of his first and more famous 'F for Freddie' Wellington bomber in which his own name had been made to the British public in *Target for To-night*. Perhaps the letter was a good omen and most pilots had one superstition or another. The damage was inspected at Predannack and they decided to take a chance and fly back to Sculthorpe on the one good engine. They arrived back at base at 18.45 hours from Predannack. It had been quite a day. They had set out at 09.30 hours.

Pick had decided that he would keep Mosquito 'F' for himself but she was out of commission as a result of the flak damage for the next three weeks. On his second flight in 'F for Freddie' after the aircraft had been repaired, he carried an interesting passenger in Lord Londonderry, formerly Minister of Air.

Over the years, Lord Londonderry and Charles Pickard had become firm friends. The previous year, and before young Nick was born, Lord Londonderry had approached Pick in an attempt to make him bend the rules. Normally Charles Pickard had a habit of making his own rules and answering the questions afterwards. On this particular occasion he denied the request of Lord Londonderry to 'be flown by Pick on an operation!' Although pressed by Lord Londonderry, with the assurance that it was simply to see what was going on at the other end, Pick felt that he could hardly be responsible if anything were to happen to such an illustrious VIP. Regretfully he had to turn the request down but the faith placed in him by Londonderry did not pass unnoticed. When his son was born on New Year's Day of 1943, Lord Londonderry was asked by Pick to be his son's godfather – an honour which Londonderry readily accepted.

For the time being, Pick had two dissatisfied operational customers on his hands. Lord Londonderry and his English sheep dog Ming. He was quite happy to fly both, or either, over the English countryside at will, but he was not prepared to take a chance over enemy territory. Thus it was that Lord Londonderry made a trip from Sculthorpe to Lyneham in Mosquito 'F for Freddie' on 25th October. From Lyneham they flew to Northolt before returning to base three hours later. Lord Londonderry expressed himself with admiration for the British aircraft industry, but he still wanted to have an operational flight.

On the second operation in the same Mosquito, a low level attack at Cleve in north-west Germany against barges on the Rhine, the aircraft was again hit and damaged by ground fire, but both engines remained intact. The end result was the same. Mosquito 'F' was off work for three weeks. For the second time, and after a three week lay-off, the aircraft was destined to carry another distinguished passenger in the navigator's seat. Wing Commander Cheshire, later to become a famous VC in the Royal Air Force, flew with Charles Pickard in a local flying and air firing exercise. They were not strangers to each other. Both had attended investitures at Buckingham Palace to be decorated on the same day.

December of 1943 was attended by inclement wintry weather, generally unsuitable for low level attacks and the next flight of Mosquito 'F' did not take place until the 21st against a target near Dieppe. The weather in England was poor from the outset, but deteriorated as the flight approached the target area. The flight was abandoned near the coast and the aircraft returned to England.

Although this flight which was aborted due to the weather may have proved a disappointment to the pilots and crews concerned, it was a warm-up for the events of the next two days when every ounce of experience would be required.

By 1943 the British were fully aware that the Germans were experimenting with both rocket and pilotless aircraft. It was reasonable to assume that the attacks would be directed against England, but apart from attacking Peenemunde on 17th August with heavy bombers of the RAF, there seemed no positive target for counter action. Peenemunde was heavily defended and the raid was only partially successful. However, information was received from a French network of spies, Reseau Agir, under Michel Hollard, on over 60 sites, together with a blueprint of a V1 launching platform, that confirmed that the secret weapon threat would be launched from Northern France.

It was still not perfectly clear in London what these new installations represented nor what would be launched from them. It was, however, clearly anticipated that the Germans were up to no good. The answer, once again, was being sought and very largely supplied by the Central Photographic Interpretation Unit at Medmenham. It will be remembered that the same unit contributed very largely to the success of the airborne attack on the radiolocation post at Bruneval. In the first six months of 1943 the whole area of Peenemunde had been covered several times by photographic Mosquitos of 540 Squadron and photographs continued to be taken of the site after bombing. On 3rd October the photographic interpreters, one of whom was Flight Officer Babington Smith of the Women's Auxiliary Air Force, observed an object looking like a small aircraft, with a wing span of approximately twenty feet and a length of approximately the same, on the edge of the airfield at Peenemunde. On the strength of this, earlier photographs were re-examined. Two more similar specimens were discovered.

The lives of Constance Babington Smith and Group Captain Pickard had touched throughout the war. Both took part in the film *Target for To-night*, both were heavily involved in the Bruneval raid, and here Flight Officer Babington Smith was intent on unravelling the secrets of the sites.

Spitfires of 541 (Photographic Reconnaissance) Squadron which were covering Northern France redoubled their efforts and, by the end of November 1943, seventy-two sites had been discovered. Each site was similar in construction to one reported in detail by the Reseau Agir and located in the middle of the Bois Carré, ten miles north-east of Abbeville. This site in the Bois Carré had been described as a 'concrete platform with a centre axis pointing directly at London'.

Squadron Leader J R H Merifield and Flight Lieutenant Baird of 540 Squadron were sent out to photograph the bomb damage in Berlin. Cloud obscured their target and they chose the airfields at Peenemunde and Zempin as an alternative.

Examination of their photographs showed an installation exactly similar to those in the Bois Carré and elsewhere. This link in the

The Mosquito and the Wheelbarrow 137

chain of photographic connection confirmed the suspicion of Photographic Intelligence. It indicated a fairly massive conglomerate of sites extending along the coastline of Northern France and to Peenemunde in the Baltic. The Germans were certainly up to no good. The evidence was ominous.

Ideally, the sites should be attacked as near to completion as possible without leaving it too late. Photographic Reconnaissance, continuously over the sites, gave a time factor of 120 days from the clearing of the site to its completion. In the months ahead, this information was of vital importance for the timing of a raid. Between the high level photographs taken by the PRU and the detailed reports made at ground level by the Reseau Agir of Michel Hollard, Medmenham turned again to its most secret department – the Model Making Section. The photographs and the measurements submitted by Robert Rubech and André Comp were translated into solid three-dimensional replicas such as a pilot would expect to find when flying at a height of thirty odd feet.

The morning of 22nd December, Air Vice-Marshal Basil Embry in charge of 2 Group, Tactical Air Force, addressed the crews of the 140th Wing who had been assembled in their conference room round Pickard. The Air Vice-Marshal was in flying kit.

Basil Embry talked to the crews in an atmosphere of tense silence and keen expectancy. He reminded the crews that a few months ago a communique had been released by the Air Ministry which referred to a large scale attack by heavy bombers of the RAF against an objective at Peenemunde in the Baltic. Forty-seven aircraft failed to return from this raid. For a very good reason the target was much more heavily defended than the RAF had anticipated and this accounted for the severe loss in men and machines.

The objective was the destruction of an experimental station where German scientists were completing work on a new type of engine. One of these machines, a type of robot-plane loaded with high explosive was already in production in the underground factories of the Reich. Secret agents in France had informed Britain of certain installations being prepared from which these infernal machines would be launched against England. The information from the agents had been confirmed by the PRU of the RAF. Hitler's secret weapon with which he held high hopes of winning the war was about to be launched against London. It was a diabolical device, indiscriminate in its powers of destruction, and aptly described by the Germans as the *Vergeltungswaffen* or revenge weapons.

As objectives, the installations were so small in area that either heavy or medium bombers flying at height would be useless. The RAF had decided that it was a job best suited to a low level attack by Mosquitos where pinpoint bombing accuracy was essential. The Air Vice-Marshal announced that the first attack against these targets would take place without further delay, and on the same day. Basil Embry stressed that it was vitally important for the attack to be successful. Dressed as he was in flying kit, the aircrews got the message. The Air Vice-Marshal was going to fly with his men, and with Basil Embry around, there would be precious few slip-ups. He was known as a very hard task master but outstandingly efficient. His very presence inspired confidence.

Basil Embry announced that 48 Mosquitos would be involved and the first 24 would be led by Group Captain Pickard. He himself would lead the second section. He had come to the conclusion early in the war that there was no synthetic method of learning about a problem and the dangers of air operations. There was only one thing for nominated leaders to do and that was to get into the air and find out for themselves. To this end, when Basil Embry took over 2 Group at the end of May 1943, he set about appointing some new commanders at station level and in Group Headquarters. He also laid down a policy that both at station level and in Group HQ, Group Captains, and above, would fly a a limited number of operations each month. This policy did not make Basil Embry the most popular man in the Royal Air Force outside 2 Group, but his policy was based on sound practical experience, and it worked.

In looking round for real operational commanders, Charles Pickard and Basil Embry came together. They had met a few times previously. Because some people had thought that Basil Embry was wrong in his policy, he was most anxious to prove that he was right. With this in mind, he nursed his senior officers as far as was possible and hand picked most of them. He would not allow a station commander to lead a show until he had carried out a certain number of operations in 2 Group.

Charles Pickard's operations had been done by night in Bomber Command and in his clandestine role. In both classes of operations, in the view of Basil Embry, he was both magnificent and supreme. This made it all the more important for Basil Embry to nurse Pick on day operations as they were so different from what he knew so well and in which he was so proficient. Pick had instructions from Basil Embry that he was *only* to fly on operations with Embry's personal permission and he need have no fear as he would be allowed a generous ration! Pick was too valuable to lose, but too valuable as a leader not to allow him to fly and inspire those under his command, and he was worth looking after. In the operations already carried out by Pick in the Mosquito, each had been selected by Basil Embry as suitable training in low level work and he had been accompanied on these flights by Embry so that his performance might be judged.

Having been briefed on the importance of the targets, the pilots then examined the model of a V1 site and acquainted themselves with the lay-out of the buildings. Accurate bomb placement and a good battering would delay any revenge attack on London. By 08.30 hours, all 48 aircraft lined the runway in pairs to the left and the right of the runway. This would expedite the time of take-off. The second pair of Mosquitos would take off when the first had moved down the runway a distance of approximately 75 yards, and these would be followed by the others at similar intervals.

The wing became airborne without trouble and formed up quickly into their various flights of six. The aircraft flew low over the channel with wisps of spray from the rough sea hitting their windscreens. The pilots could only hope that stray sea-gulls would keep their heads down. The shock of a sea-gull hitting the leading edge of a Mosquito at speed was enough to crack the wing spar.

The first ground check was a lonely farmhouse on the cliffs of the French coast two miles west of Criel. The farmhouse was surrounded by a square shaped wood making it easy to recognise. From there, the route led from Dieppe to Treport where they turned south. Dieppe would be left a few miles on their starboard side as they flew down the valley south of Treport. There was a river to cross as they followed the valley; up, over, and into a smaller one with higher ground to the south of the second valley where they would meet a road which they followed for a few miles. This road wound through the peaceful orchards of Normandy, so far removed from the object of the Mosquitos' exercise. The target area lay on the left hand side of the road.

They flew in echelon starboard and in very tight formation, hugging the ground at zero feet. The constant change of course would be deceptive to the enemy and a flight at zero feet would help to fox the enemy radar. The flight continued at 270 miles per hour, well within the limits of the Mosquito, but allowing for greater bombing accuracy. Approaching the target area, they levelled off at thirty feet, eyes skinned for the buildings and lay-out with which they had all made themselves familiar before take-off, and straight ahead lay the curious set-up. Forty-eight angry Mosquitos plastered the area in consecutive waves with devastating accuracy. When they left, without looking back, the set-up looked even more curious. Hitler's secret weapon had received its first punch in the bread-basket from the Mosquitos of the 140th Wing, Tactical Air Force, and they didn't like it. No, they didn't like it at all.

Christmas was due in a few days time. 'Peace on Earth and Goodwill towards Men', but there should be no rest for the wicked. The wicked are in need of help. They must be helped to mend their manners. The Mosquitos of the 140th Wing returned once more on 23rd December with Charles Pickard again at the helm on another very successful manners mending mission. Thus began the Mosquito attacks against the rocket launching pads in Northern France which were to delay the indiscriminate bombing of London by the V1's. The revenge weapon of the Germans was a sword of two edges. It had the same characteristics as a man spending a penny into the wind.

The initial and continued attacks by the Mosquitos delayed the V1 rockets being launched against England until June of the following year. The contribution made by Michel Hollard, backed by the work of the Photographic Reconnaissance Units of the Royal Air Force and the modelling section at Medmenham contributed immeasurably towards the saving of countless lives in London with the possible deterioration of morale among the entire British people.

Later, Winston Churchill was to pay his own tribute to the agents involved, including the French, Poles and other nationals, who risked their lives to save England from its peril. His account of the postponement and eventual defeat of the V1 was summed up when he wrote in *The Second World War*:

> Our Intelligence had played a vital part. The size and performance of the weapon, and the intended scale of attack, were known to us in excellent time. This enabled our fighters to be made ready. The launching sites and the storage caverns were found, enabling our bombers to delay the attack and mitigate its violence. Every known means of getting information was employed, and it was pieced together with great skill. To all sources, many of whom worked amid deadly danger, and some of whom will be for ever unknown to us, I pay my tribute.

General Eisenhower was no less direct. In his *Crusade in Europe* (Heinemann, 1949) he wrote:

> It seems likely that if the Germans had succeeded in perfecting and using these new weapons six months earlier than they did, our invasion of Europe would have proved exceedingly difficult, perhaps impossible. I feel sure that if they had succeeded in using these weapons over a six months period, and particularly if they had made the Portsmouth/Southampton area one of their principal targets, 'Overlord' might have been written off.

The Germans had, in fact, sustained a major defeat. Their last trump card had been played, and they had lost. Hitler's high hopes lay in ruins in the fields of Northern France.

CHAPTER NINE

Pickard of Picardy

Early in 1944 further news filtered through France. The information was accompanied by accurate drawings of a large prison, surrounded by a high wall. In common with the V1 launching pads, the object of the information was in Northern France: Amiens.

The Somme area of France and the plains of Picardy have known the worst ravages of war spanning two generations. The river Somme flows gently across the plains of Picardy and there can be few soldiers from either war who have not heard with apprehension the names of St Valery, Arras, Abbeville and Amiens. The unbelievable destruction and the loss of men who fought for a few hundred yards of territory, denuded of living trees and living creatures, was covered by a sea of mud, a plague of lice, and two armies facing each other in the grimmest possible conditions in the war to end all wars of 1914–1918.

By the beginning of 1944 the old order had mercifully ended and occupied France could only hope to survive by a battle of wits. To this end, the French worked with no less dedication or courage in the patient role of the Underground. If caught, the penalties were less than human.

Across the country, Underground networks extended from the channel to the Mediterranean. In the forefront once more were the patriots in Northern France, aided by men, women and equipment flown out from England by the airmen from Tempsford. Sabotage took place wherever the blow would be most decisive as arms and equipment were built up for the anticipated day of liberation. Traitors abounded and the gaunt, grey and forbidding prison of Amiens became filled with men of valour who had slipped by the wayside. Their battle was always with an unseen enemy, their only reward the quickest possible liberation of France.

From a distance, the ancient town of Amiens has two notable features – the beautiful cathedral and the abominable prison. Both rise high over the surrounding flat countryside. The one provides for voluntary sinners, the other for incautious criminals.

It is a paradox of war that a patriot becomes a criminal in the eyes of the opposition. To this thinking, the Gestapo had subscribed for the past five years. The patriotic French in the Somme area who were caught in the act and those who were given away by collaborators for a price, found that it was a very short step to the unhallowed ground of Amiens Prison where their world was confined by a very high wall topped with broken glass.

Most active in the Underground network which comprised the Amiens district, known as 'Sosies', was a trio of formidable men. The Ponchardier brothers, Dominique and Pierre, administered the area with an efficiency allied to secrecy which defied all attempts by German Counter Intelligence to put an end to the network. In their dangerous and desperate work they were ably assisted by a gentleman known as 'Pepe' who was a very tough individual indeed.

Dominique Ponchardier had been responsible for the zone which had been occupied by the enemy since 1940. Pierre looked after the zone beyond the demarcation line of his brother. The northern zone included the Channel coastline and this demanded constant attention. This particular area had been entrusted by Dominique to his very good and reliable friend Riviere who, although himself a Captain of a frigate, had voluntarily placed himself under the orders of Dominique. The coastal area under Riviere was known as MA 1 – Marine 1, and Riviere's right hand man was Pepe.

Pepe had been a confirmed communist. As such he had taken part in the Spanish war. His communistic leanings were intense and this convinced him that participation in a war was the correct way of expressing his ideals. He went to war in Spain for his ideals. By the end of the Spanish Civil War his ideals had suffered a rude awakening and he became thoroughly disappointed in his communist masters and with the organisation. Without further ado, he left the party. Always the supreme idealist, Pepe did not have to search far in 1940 to take up the gauntlet which the Germans threw down to loyal Frenchmen, idealists, and men of energy. Pepe was a man with an excess of energy. For the dangerous and exacting work required by the Underground networks in France, Pepe was an experienced and ideal leader.

The Ponchardier brothers and Pepe headed the Mezieres-Charleville network which they had started as far back as October 1940. Pepe was the most suitable choice of the Ponchardier brothers as he knew the area well, had many very good friends on whom he could rely and was such a crack shot that he was known affectionately as Pistol to his friends. The organisation concerned itself with sabotage of the German war effort, and the escape of those connected with the organisation who were being hounded by the Gestapo. Pepe subscribed to the view that nothing succeeds like excess. When Germany declared war on Russia he wasted no time in forming an armed group of Communists which concentrated its efforts in the Somme and Seine-Inferieure regions.

In the middle of 1943, a trainload of the Wehrmacht carried men who were going on leave. At Miremont on the Paris-Lille line this trainload of fighting fit men had a rude shock awaiting them. Another train carrying troops and tanks to the Eastern Front had made an unscheduled stop at a moment most inconvenient to the train bearing down on it from the north. With a rending of metal the fast moving train from the north telescoped into the stationary east bound train, and the east bound train went west. Among the ensuing debris lay one hundred dead SS troops and NCO's, ninety SS officers, and one SS Division General.

A few weeks later another packed troop train was heading for the Eastern Front. Travelling at speed in the middle of the night, the train approached a bend on the line at Frireules on the Treport-Abbeville line. The train very suddenly became de-railed spilling hundreds of German soldiery at the side of the railway line. When the dust had settled, two hundred Germans were found dead and over 400 on the severely injured list. Three other derailed trains were to follow with equally devastating damage and five trainloads of troops were marked up to the work of one man in the Ponchardier organisation, Jean Beaurin.

Jean Beaurin was a specialist. He specialised in de-railing trains. His luck held out for a surprising length of time before he was caught by the Gestapo and consigned to the old prison of Amiens towards the end of 1943. As Pepe's deputy, the loss to the organisation in the Picardy region was grievous.

At the time, Jean Beaurin was 20 years of age. For his tender

(Top) 'Ming' leading the way to fly as Pickard's 'Observer'.

(Bottom) Evening departure.

F/Lt. J. A. Broadley adjusts Pickard's Mae West before take-off.

The model of Amiens prison used for briefing.

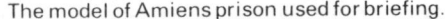

(Right) Mosquitos over the target in the low level attack on Amiens prison.

(Right) Smoke pouring from the damaged prison.

(Right) A view of the damaged prison and prison wall.

(Left) The breach in the south side of the outer wall of Amiens prison.

(Below) A reconnaissance photograph taken on March 23rd, 1944. The escape breach in the wall can be seen in the bottom right corner.

years he had learned his trade of de-railing railway engines with alacrity attended by success. Pepe, Jean Beaurin and Dominique Ponchardier had an unwritten agreement among themselves. If any of them were to be picked up by the Germans, the others would move heaven and earth to help the less fortunate one to escape. The prison at Amiens was a formidable obstacle to their escape plans. By December of 1943, twelve other members of Pepe's entourage, operating out of the Mers-les-Bains region, including their leader 'le Sec', had been shot inside the prison. Jean Beaurin awaited the same fate with precious little hope of his friends being able to help.

Pepe had an assistant called Maurice Holleville who had been nick-named 'the Vicar of Montparnasse'. Holleville had a peculiar, dignified, priest-like gait, and walked with his hands out. Together they were on their way to discuss the possibility of attacking Amiens prison with another of their group by the name of Serge. The meeting was to take place in the Beaulot Cafe, just behind Amiens station. It was perhaps ironical that they should plan to meet behind the station as the subject under discussion was their former railway expert and the means whereby he could be released. Serge had kept one half of the map of Amiens Prison and Pepe had the other. Three minutes before the pair arrived at the cafe, Serge was arrested. Holleville had a priest-like intuition as they approached the cafe. He warned Pepe at the last moment and his chief only just managed to escape the trap which had been set for him. Together they walked past the cafe.

Now into the month of January, ill fortune seemed to be stalking the Ponchardier organisation. Jean Beaurin was in Amiens Prison and was being joined by Serge who no doubt had been caught with the map of the prison in his pocket. One of Pepe's men, Eugene, had launched an attack on the prison at Saint Quentin in an operation very similar to the one being planned against the prison at Amiens. The attack was a complete fiasco and resulted in the Germans re-doubling their vigilance everywhere. The loss of Pepe's twelve men in December only added to their wounds and their worry. The map of half the Amiens Prison which must surely have been found when Serge was searched would only serve to make an attack on the prison almost insurmountable. The final blow of ill fortune was struck when Maurice Holleville, the Vicar of Montparnasse, was also caught. The good 'Vicar' was caught in a simple matter of trying to 'acquire' ration cards from the Town Hall. Those who lived a clandestine existence to the point of being non-existent, could hardly register for ration cards. Man must eat and the Vicar was caught. He was sent to join Beaurin, Serge and the others inside the grim walls at Amiens. The score, in favour of the Germans, was mounting rapidly. The opportunity of attacking the prison to carry out their promise to their friends was fading fast.

Even before the final disaster with the Vicar, Ponchardier and Pepe had decided to abandon their plan. Allowing that Serge had somehow managed to destroy the desperately incriminating map of his half of the Amiens Prison plan, Serge was also aware of the proposed scheme to attack the prison. Loyal in the extreme though they were, the Gestapo had means of making the most loyal speak. The means were none too delicate. Both agreed that it would be utter madness to go ahead with a combined attack by the Underground.

Pepe was by now very much under suspicion himself and he decided that discretion was the better part of valour. Prudently he made himself scarce by withdrawing to the country. He was not to be allowed to lick his wounds for long. He was sought out by the mother of Jean Beaurin and the father of Maurice Holleville. Both pleaded with not a little anguish for Pepe to do something to save their children. He gave his word that something would be done and lost no time in contacting Dominique Ponchardier.

Urged by the pleadings of both parents, and mindful of the unwritten promise made in the earlier days, he reminded Ponchardier that they had promised to help each other . . . even if it cost them their lives.

Dominique Ponchardier was a man of great strength, cunning and resource. He knew that his network had been infiltrated, the planned ground attack against the prison now known to the Germans, and the news had leaked out to him from the prison that Jean Beaurin was to be shot on 19th February with more than 100 others. They were in desperate straits which called for desperate measures.

He summoned his Deputy, Riviere, put him fully in the picture, and discussed the situation at length and from every angle. The position seemed hopeless and Ponchardier began to regret the folly of their earlier agreement which could now result in his entire network being wiped out. He was, however, very much a man of his word and no-one crossed swords or broke their word to a man like Pepe.

Dominique Ponchardier reluctantly had to admit that there was no possible way in which the prison could be attacked from the ground without countless casualties on both sides and very little chance of success. If it could not be attacked from the ground, he was left with only one alternative. The alternative offered unknown and untried tactics and was frightening in its possible implications.

He sent plans to London through his network, consisting of the lay-out of Amiens Prison, the position of the German guards in the jail, eating habits, the height and width of the surrounding wall, the location of the defence gun emplacements and the number of each man manning the guns. Report followed report with mystifying regularity in London, all concerned with Amiens Prison. The Intelligence Service received them without comment in the knowledge that the sender, Dominique Ponchardier, would not waste his time on frivolous information. However, Ponchardier bided his time as he baffled London with numerous reports on the lay-out of the prison. Each report consisted of remarkable detail, and London waited. The cunning of Ponchardier was apparent to no-one and his hand was strengthened when two officers in the Intelligence Service were caught by the Germans and quickly found their way into the grim fortress of Amiens. It was the trump card Ponchardier had awaited.

Ponchardier was on very good terms with the top men in the British Intelligence Service who had promised him their utmost support. During his stay in London between two missions he had also met Group Captain Pickard. Early in February he sent a message to London requesting the help of the Royal Air Force for an attack on Amiens prison as 'it just so happened' that the Royal Air Force had plans of Amiens jail already in their hands!! It was one of many coups organised by Ponchardier which 'just so happened'. Ponchardier was well known as a thoroughly organised happener.

The top secret request from France passed through the normal channels until it was received by Coningham, the Commander-in-Chief of the 2nd Tactical Air Force. Without delay Coningham contacted Air Vice Marshal Basil Embry, Air Officer Commanding No 2 Group, for an urgent consultation. It had to be established whether Basil Embry felt that his Mosquitos were capable of carrying out an operation to release 700 odd prisoners, most of whom were French Resistance Movement patriots awaiting trial and death in Amiens Prison. The Mosquitos had already proved their worth in pinpoint bombing accuracy on the V1 launching sites, but the bombing of a prison was a new concept where so many friendly lives could be at stake. Basil Embry was cautious in his approach, but gave it as his opinion that he thought it would be possible. First, the full implications of such an operation would have to be examined in minute detail before giving a definite answer. Careful investigation followed without time being lost before a full and reasonably accurate assessment could be made. The attack could be successful, but would not be possible without a certain loss among the lives of the prisoners. To this stern warning the answer came back from the prisoners at Amiens. They would prefer to die by British bombs rather than German bullets. With this macabre statement of fact from Amiens, the planning went ahead.

The first urgent steps taken by Basil Embry were to have the prison photographed and modelled by the modelling section. He next called for advice from someone who could elaborate on the detailed particulars of the internal and external construction of the prison and its surrounding wall, the internal lay-out with every possible detail on the cells, the locks and the doors, and the regular prison routine. The information which had already been received from Dominique Ponchardier by Intelligence quickly helped to bridge this gap.

The prison was in the form of a cross surrounded by a brick wall twenty feet high, three feet thick, and the wall liberally topped with broken glass. The prison was heavily guarded by specially selected troops who were accommodated inside the prison in separate buildings, but adjoining the prison itself. These would rank as top priority to help nullify the attention of gun-happy guards.

The building was located outside the town of Amiens on the road to Albert which is a long, straight highway, fortunately lacking in obstructions and providing a well-defined lead to the target for a low level attack. Lee Howard, the photographer in the lone Mosquito of the Operational Film Production Unit piloted by Tony Wickham which accompanied the raid, was later to describe the prison as 'the last door on the right as you enter the town from Bapaume'.

Technical advice on the amount of exposure to breach the thick prison walls and force the locks on cells and prison doors had to be obtained. This constituted one of the most critical assessments in the entire operation. Too little would fail to breach the walls and sever the locks. Too much would result in excessive casualties.

It was decided to breach the outer wall in two places to create an exit at either end. This would anticipate any obstructions being placed across the prison yard by the Germans. An attempt must also be made to eliminate as many of the guards as possible at the beginning of the attack and this could best be done by destroying the part of the buildings in which the guards were quartered. From the information already received, it was of paramount importance to note that the prisoners normally assembled for lunch shortly before noon. Of equal importance, the guards were assembled for lunch at the same hour in their own buildings which would make the task of eliminating as many guards as possible with a few well placed bombs easier and more effective. The time selected for the attack was precisely 12 noon. The date would be any day after the 10th of February and before the 19th and this was entirely subject to the adverse weather conditions which covered England and Europe at that time.

The plans were approved and completed by the 8th February but the possible death of the prisoners who had contributed so much to the Allied cause weighed very heavily on the mind of Basil Embry. It was a hateful responsibility which he had to carry alone. The burden was made no easier for him by having to sit on the ground and watch others put his plan into execution.

On the afternoon of 8th February, Basil Embry flew to RAF Hunsdon where 140 Wing was stationed to brief Charles Pickard, the Commanding Officer, and his Wing Leader. Hunsdon is not far from Salisbury Hall, the birthplace of the immaculate Mosquito which was used in the historic attack on Amiens Prison, and of these, eighteen would be selected from 487 Squadron, Royal New

Zealand Air Force, 464 Squadron, Royal Australian Air Force, and 21 Squadron, Royal Air Force. The Mosquitos would receive close support from twelve Typhoons based at Westhampnett. The Typhoons had to rendezvous with the Mosquitos over Littlehampton, escort the Mosquitos on the way to the target area and take care of the German fighter aerodrome at Glisy, a short distance due west of Amiens and close by the river Somme.

The first six Mosquitos were to break the prison walls and destroy the German guardhouse. This was left to 487 Squadron. The second formation from 464 Squadron was detailed to place their bombs against the walls of the prison, and the third in 21 Squadron was to be in reserve. 21 Squadron was being held back for the moment of truth. If the outside walls were not properly breached or if no-one was seen to be escaping which would indicate that the cell locks had not been successfully forced, 21 Squadron would deliver the final coup de grace and carry out the macabre alternative requested by the French. The alternative was horrifying in the extreme and too grim to contemplate.

A few, but not all the prisoners, had been warned of the impending attack. The utmost secrecy had to be maintained to prevent the Germans being forewarned with disastrous results to the attacking force and the prisoners themselves.

With little time left on hand to select a very experienced leader in low level work, Basil Embry had elected to lead the raid himself. Charles Pickard was to fly as his deputy leader and he was left to choose his crews, and brief them with the help of the model of the prison which was left with great secrecy at Hunsdon. Basil Embry was due to meet Sir Trafford Leigh-Mallory on the following day, the 9th, at Hartford Bridge where Leigh-Mallory was inspecting 137 Wing.

The operation had originally been called 'Renovate' but this had been changed to 'Operation Jericho' for very apt reasons, and it was on this subject that Leigh-Mallory discussed developments at length with Basil Embry. In detail the plans were made known to Leigh-Mallory. He listened with grave interest to every word as the magnitude of the task and the need for experienced leaders and crews was emphasised by Basil Embry, but passed no comment.

'Who is leading the raid?' he asked when Embry had finished.

'I am, Sir', replied Embry, but there was still no comment.

Basil Embry took his leave, not without a certain feeling of misgiving. Tomorrow was the 10th. Time was running short and there was only eight days in hand, with everything now dependent upon the weather. The raid *could* take place within 48 hours.

The feeling of misgiving which Basil Embry felt as he took his leave of Air Chief Marshal Sir Trafford Leigh-Mallory was not misplaced. The same evening, back at his headquarters, a signal was received from his Commander-in-Chief, addressed to him personally. It left no room for doubt.

The message read, 'ON NO ACCOUNT, repeat NO ACCOUNT, are you to fly on operation discussed this afternoon. Acknowledge.'

In view of the time factor and finding a suitably experienced substitute for himself, this was a bitter blow. The operation had been one of the most carefully planned of the war at that time. The requirements of leading a low level attack varied from those of normal bombing operations in which there was no substitute for experience. Basil Embry had selected Charles Pickard as his deputy leader for the raid. He was the first to admit that Pickard was supreme in both his high level bombing and clandestine roles, but he also knew that Pick lacked experience in leading low level attacks which had their own basic rules.

It was a basic general rule in 2 Group's Mosquito operations, by day, that the formations went in and then got the hell out of it at ground level with full throttle. *Never go round again.* The attacks against the rocket launching pads had proved that enemy fighters presented little or no problem when the Mosquito was flown at tree-top height on full throttle. The main occupational hazard came from light flak, arguing with a tree or some other such obstruction. The total number of low level attacks in which Charles Pickard had taken part before Amiens did not exceed six. On these particular operations he was accompanied by Basil Embry in his schoolmaster capacity of nursing his valuable senior station commanders in any new role.

Before the eventful meeting with Sir Trafford Leigh-Mallory, it had been arranged that Basil Embry would lead the attack on Amiens, with Charles Pickard as his deputy coming in with the third and fateful wave of 21 Squadron. The decision of whether the raid had been a success was to be left to Pickard. If not, the prison and the prisoners would be dealt an irreparable blow.

The communication from the Commander-in-Chief placed Basil Embry in an invidious position and he was faced with a difficult decision. He telephoned his immediate commander, Air Marshal Sir Arthur Coningham who was commander of the 2nd Tactical Air Force, and explained that the crews had already been briefed and to change the leader at the last moment was asking for trouble.

He replied, 'Basil, I agree with you, but please don't argue over this one. The C-in-C is *quite* adamant over this and it will do no good to raise the matter with him.'

There the matter ended. It left Basil Embry with one of the most difficult decisions to make in his illustrious flying career.

He did not feel that his friend Charles Pickard had the necessary experience of daytime low level operations to lead, yet he had appointed Pick as his deputy commander with a clear cut task to fulfil. If, at this late hour, he were to appoint one of his other squadron commanders with more experience on the type of raid ahead, it would be tantamount to indicating that he did not have the confidence in Pick as a leader, causing a possible hurt beyond repair. There was no possible alternative. The three squadrons were on alert and in readiness. They had been brought to as fine a pitch as possible for the unique and historical raid ahead. Charles Pickard and his inseparable navigator Alan Broadley must lead the attack. The die was cast. To make doubly sure that Basil Embry did not, for once, disobey an order, the Commander-in-Chief summoned him to report to the Headquarters of Fighter Command the following morning. He was going to make sure Basil Embry did not fly.

The concentrated training of the three squadrons at Hunsdon had not been without humour in the abysmal weather. The long runway had a peculiar and unsatisfactory dip in the middle, and not all the pilots were thoroughly acquainted with the magnificent Mosquito. The adverse winter weather did nothing to help a series of bent, buckled and broken Mosquitos when landing or taxi-ing. Any damage to his precious aircraft infuriated Pickard, gentle though he was, to such an extent that he had a very large and prominent notice placed in the crew room.

Picard of Picardy

It read, simply, 'The next person to prang a Mosquito through finger trouble will be posted to the bloodiest job in the Air Force.'

The pilots read and digested the notice in fear and trembling. Charles Pickard was a man of his word.

Life is full of surprises, ironical though they may be. The day after the terrible warning was issued and placed in prominence in the crew room, a lone Mosquito dragged a bent tail wheel back to the tarmac. The pilot stepped down. He was Group Captain Charles Pickard. Without daring to smile, little did the other pilots think that Pick had consigned himself to 'the bloodiest job in the Air Force.'

The attacking force at Hunsdon stood by. Everything was in readiness and the crews were confined to camp. The weather continued on its non-operational way with low cloud, frost and snow. The prison at Amiens awaited.

The weather continued to deteriorate after the 10th, although a slight improvement was forecast by the 14th. A message was sent out by radio to Ponchardier to ask him to stand by for midday on any day after the 15th. February is a poor month in which to make accurate predictions on a weather forecast and it took a turn for the worse. Consternation grew on both sides of the channel as snow fell heavily in freezing temperatures throughout Europe and Britain on 16th and 17th of February. The date of the 19th drew dangerously close when the Germans were due to carry out the execution of over 100 prisoners. The weather cancelled all air operations on both days, but all personnel at RAF Hunsdon were confined to camp and on standby.

The morning of the 18th began with little better promise. England lay under a blanket of snow. Low cloud in the form of a ground mist drifted across the bleak airfield and reports from the Meteorological Office were in no way encouraging. South Eastern England was in no better case than the totally bleak outlook at Hunsdon, and further snowstorms were predicted. If the prisoners were to be saved, it was now or never, regardless of the conditions which would have grounded most aircraft. Further delay was out of the question, and Basil Embry stood by with Charles Pickard as the crews from the eighteen Mosquitos were called to the briefing room in the cold, grey morning light at 8 o'clock.

In addition to the eighteen Mosquitos directly involved in the raid, an extra Mosquito of the Operational Film Production Unit was on standby to be flown by Flight Lieutenant Tony Wickham with Lee Howard in the navigator's seat and his cameras at the ready. This particular Mosquito was closely guarded and much cared for by the Operational Film Production Unit. Apart from a couple of Bostons and ageing Ansons, with occasionally a Mitchell or two, it was the only really good aircraft which regularly flew on operations. The members of this unit had been warned that this particular Mosquito could not, and would not, be replaced if lost. This tended to make life difficult all round. Oddly, it was the navigator/cinematographer himself who decided whether conditions were favourable for OFPU work. It was his duty to make an intelligent guess as to whether the aircraft should be risked on a particular operation to produce a successful cine film. He was under instructions from the Air Ministry, to which he directly belonged, to indicate to the Commanding Officer of the station that he was sorry, the weather, in his opinion, was unsuitable and the OFPU Mosquito should not be sent. Lee Howard, now filing in with the others to the briefing room at Hunsdon, remembered well the amount of joy he received from the Group Captain at Marham when, as an indifferent flight sergeant, he refused to fly on a particular trip, or to allow his precious aircraft to be sent. The life of the Group Captain was only saved by him not knowing how to faint and have apoplexy at the same time. The Group Captain was on his way to bursting.

The weather looked very dark and threatening, with a sky packed full of snow, as they filed into the briefing room. Apart from Basil Embry and Charles Pickard, no-one had any idea what the operation entailed. Most of the crews expected that the weather conditions would make it just another wasted trip to the briefing room, a cold walk in the snow, before being sent back to the doubtful heat of their quarters. The briefing room appeared to be unusually heavily guarded, with a substantially more-than-usual quota of frozen-stiff RAF police types. The crews were subjected to a scrutiny amounting to embarrassment which made some think that the Air Chief Marshal's daughter must have been molested without permission. No such luck awaited them in the briefing room.

The stamping of cold feet and the idle hum of speculation ended when Charles Pickard entered the room and walked to a table on which a large sealed box stood. The box had already defied the attempts by the more inquisitive to establish the nature of its contents. A few moments later the crews came to attention as a determined but inscrutable Basil Embry strode in to take his place beside their commanding officer, Charles Pickard. The proceedings were opened by the Air Vice-Marshal with a note of caution. He added to the feeling of strict security which the heavily guarded briefing room had already inspired by asking that the operation about to take place should continue to remain top secret, if weather conditions prevented it on the appointed day. Pausing to allow his words to be digested, his eyes piercing the crews in turn, Basil Embry removed the outer covering of the wooden box. It revealed a model, built accurately to scale by his modelling section, on a base approximately four feet square, of Amiens Prison. The model showed very simply and clearly the cross-like structure of the building and how the salient features would appear to an aircraft flying at 500 feet at a distance of four miles.

The crews moved closer to examine the model and memorise the details. It was stark in its simplicity and more stark in its implication.

Charles Pickard commenced the briefing. He explained exactly what the target was and the reasons for it being attacked. Surprise and accuracy were equally essential to the success of the raid, and they could only hope that the weather would clear. The necessity to carry out the raid as soon as possible was explained to the crews with the grim information that over 100 French patriots would be executed the following morning unless the raid was a success. The tension in the room mounted when he used a phrase which few of the crews would ever forget.

'And they have told us that they would rather be blown up by British bombs than shot by the Nazis.'

This simple statement of fact which had been conveyed to the British authorities served to fortify the assembled aircrews with a sense of resolute dedication. Their worst enemy at the moment was the abominable weather.

Having covered the general lay-out of the prison, the urgency of the mission and the observation of the heroic prisoners, Charles

Pickard moved on to the details of the attack. The crews were to be given an opportunity to study the model more thoroughly at the end of the briefing.

The first squadron to attack, taking care of the German guardrooms and the outer wall would be 487, Royal New Zealand Air Force. The second wave, in which he would fly himself, would be 464 Squadron, Royal Australian Air Force, and 21 Squadron, Royal Air Force, would stand by to flatten the prison if the prisoners were not seen to be escaping.

Pick announced that he would make his own bombing run as the last aircraft in 464 Squadron. This would give him the maximum possible time in which to drop his bombs, circle the target if necessary, and assess the success of the raid. Everything depended upon split-second timing and accurate navigation up to the target. In this they would be helped by approaching along the long straight road from Albert. To deceive the enemy as to the exact target, the aircraft would fly north of Amiens, by way of Doullens, before turning south-east for Albert, from where they would pick up the long and very straight road to Amiens and the prison. Subject to good visibility, the prison should be seen standing gaunt and stark against the snow covered ground.

Much to the disappointment of the British crews in 21 Squadron, they would stand by for the message from Pick. A call over the RT of 'Green, green, green' would indicate that the first two waves had not been successful and 21 Squadron must carry out their terrible task. If the raid had been successful, he would call out 'Red, red, red. The oranges are ripe!' On receipt of this code message, every aircraft must high-tail it back to England at low level and in the shortest possible time. The twelve Typhoons from 198 Squadron which were to accompany the Mosquitos and give fighter protection would leave the Mosquitos on the approach to Amiens and make for the airfield at Glisy to discourage any enemy fighter aircraft from taking off. Their job would also be complete when they heard the code message from Pick and they were to leave the airfield at Glisy without further delay.

To help with the accuracy of the bombing, the approach speed of the Mosquitos would be reduced to 270 miles per hour. After bombing, it was every man for himself. Pick ended the briefing session as the crews listened with rapt attention. Before leaving the pilots to study the model of the prison more fully and the navigators to discuss navigation details with Alan Broadley, Pick looked round the room at his hand picked experienced crews. His final words to them all were to be strangely prophetic.

In the silence he concluded, 'It's a death or glory job, boys.'

The gentle giant from Yorkshire left in the company of Basil Embry who had been present throughout. Before doing so, he asked the crew of the Film Production Unit Mosquito to meet him in his office. For Basil Embry, the briefing had been a terrible anti-climax to his own plans. The Air Vice-Marshal was able to sense the feeling of elation the briefing had caused while he, perforce, stood idly by. The raid which he had planned in such minute detail must go ahead without his active participation. He was never cast in the role of the idle onlooker and the ominous, grey, snow filled clouds did nothing to improve his spirit. He took his leave of Charles Pickard to attend to other matters concerning 2 Group.

Charles Pickard returned immediately to his office where Flight Lieutenant Tony Wickham and Lee Howard of the film unit Mosquito awaited him. At 10 o'clock, with little improvement being apparent in the weather, he made a quick check with 2 Group Headquarters. The met office reports indicated no improvement over southern England, but prospects over the channel were thought to be brighter and these conditions should hold out for the target area in Northern France. Until the improving conditions could be verified, it was suggested that a short postponement might be advisable. With only two hours left to keep their rendezvous with Ponchardier and the Underground workers outside the prison, Pick felt that nothing was to be gained by delaying matters further. His main concern was a postponement leading to a cancellation of the entire trip and, with time running out, there was too much at stake. The operation would go ahead as planned and he called the aircraft to readiness.

He invited the crew of the film unit Mosquito into his office as the other Mosquitos were being swept clear of snow, topped up with fuel, and loaded with their bombs by the armourers. He addressed his remarks to Tony Wickham in a very matter-of-fact manner.

'If by any chance anything happens to me on the raid, as I expect to be going round two or three times, I would like you to take over if you see the prisoners making a break for it and you haven't heard my call signal. I want you to assess how successful the first two squadrons have been as you fly over and photograph the damage.'

Lest any mistakes were made in the excitement over the target, Lee Howard wrote down the two separate call signs to be kept handy for immediate reference if they did not hear the call from Pick. Tony Wickham was a very likeable and amusing young man. As they left Pickard's office to attend to last minute details, he turned to Lee Howard who was acting as his navigator/photographer on this particular operation.

'As if I haven't got enough trouble, nursemaiding some filmic twit on a conducted tour of a squalid dump, I now have to be secretary, chief cook and bottle washer to old Freddie. Our CO has always been near the mark when he says . . . "there is always a bloody something!" '

His CO and the 'old Freddie' to whom Tony Wickham referred, was then an energetic 28 years old. They walked across the snow covered tarmac and clambered aboard happily to attend to business.

The other aircrews were already strapped in their aircraft warming their engines with the deep throated Rolls-Royce Merlin engines both warming and re-assuring. The weather had not improved. Visibility extended no further than half way down the runway to the peculiar and unsettling dip in the middle. The crews remained at their controls with their minds still full of doubt. All doubt was dispelled when a staff car drew up beside a Mosquito bearing the significant letter 'F' and Group Captain Pickard stepped out. Unlikely though the conditions seemed, the raid was going ahead. They were definitely for the 'Off'.

Squadron Leader W R C 'Dick' Sugden was flying with his own CO, Bob Iredale, in 464 Squadron. Dick was later to record that it was possibly the most atrocious weather he had ever encountered. To keep straight on the take-off run, climb immediately into snow and formate as closely as possible in a blinding snow storm, was a task which few of the pilots on the raid had ever experienced. In the event, four of the Mosquitos became detached from the rest of the wing as they flew to rendezvous with the Typhoons over

Picard of Picardy

Littlehampton. Separated from the main body, they were unable to regain contact, and the dejected pilots had to make an about turn on instruments in the hope of making base. The total Mosquito attacking force was now reduced to fourteen aircraft before the Channel was crossed.

The Typhoons fared little better. Of the original twelve which took off from 198 Squadron, four became detached in the heavy cloud and snow and had to return to base. The total force of thirty aircraft was reduced to twenty-two before a break in the weather and a glimmer of light could be seen half way across the Channel.

The problems were not yet over for the same Dick Sugden as the first break appeared in the weather. Coming out of the cloud and snow he could see a Mosquito weaving immediately in front of him, so close that a collision seemed inevitable. Tense with the ordeal of overcoming the well nigh impossible, without thinking, he grabbed for his RT.

In a voice fraught with anxiety he called out, 'Get the hell out of it, you bastard!'

The offending Mosquito obligingly did. As it veered away, Dick was able to see the identification letter on the side of the Mosquito. It read 'F'.

Bursting into sunlight, Dick Sugden had few illusions about his future as a pilot in the RAF when they returned to base. He had committed three cardinal sins. He had told his CO to go to hell; he had called him a bastard; and most grievous of all, he had broken radio silence on the approach to the French coastline. In the meantime, the question of his future would have to wait, but knowing the strict obedience to the rules of 'F for Freddie' whilst in the air, Dick was sure of one thing. His future as a pilot in the RAF was null and void.

With the snow and cloud behind them, the aircraft headed for the Dieppe-le Treport road over which they had so recently flown in the attacks against the launching pads. They were now in familiar territory if looking slightly different under its mantle of snow. Flying to the north of Amiens, they made for Doullens, hugging the contours of the ground along the Somme Valley and the flat plains of Picardy. The Typhoons covered the Mosquitos like angry hornets looking for trouble.

A further casualty was to fall to the leading New Zealand squadron. Before the target was reached, Mosquito 'Q for Queenie' being flown by the irrepressible Flight Lieutenant B. D. 'Tich' Hanafin had smoke trailing from the port engine. The propeller was feathered and Tich continued to maintain his position in the flight on one engine. The Mosquito responded remarkably well and he hoped that the cooling effect of the outer air would remedy the trouble. Closer to the target he decided to try and re-start the engine to give him increased stability on the run-in and maximum power with bombs away. Ten miles from Amiens and with the target almost in sight Queenie was again in serious trouble with the defective port engine causing the aircraft to vibrate.

Tich did not wish to jeopardise the split-second timing of the attack upon which the two leading squadrons depended and he pulled out to drop his bombs in open country, feather the engine once more, and make tracks for England on one engine. His troubles were only beginning. The German defence guns had now been alerted and Queenie was on her own without the protection of the Typhoons which were, even then, making their way to take care of the fighter station at Glisy. The ailing Mosquito was hit by ground flak and 'Tich' received some ragged shrapnel in his neck, causing him intense pain. The wound bled profusely and his right side was fast becoming paralysed. His navigator gave him a shot of morphine which helped ease the pain but did not improve the paralysis. Assisted by his navigator, it was only through sheer guts and utter determination that the aircraft was flown across the channel. 'Q for Queenie' made a successful emergency landing in Sussex.

The remaining thirteen aircraft settled down to the job ahead. Of these, only nine would be directly involved in the first two attacks before a decision was made on the success, or otherwise, of the attack and 21 Squadron, in the rear, had now been reduced to an active striking force of four. The remaining two in 21 Squadron had aborted due to weather.

The clock on the cathedral at Amiens showed 12 noon exactly. The ground was frozen and white, with visibility good. Dominique Ponchardier anxiously awaited as he walked unobtrusively with his men in the vicinity of the prison. Since the news had been received to expect the raid on any day after the 12th the loyal group of

French had patrolled the area each day at the appointed hour. Accommodation for the escaping prisoners had been organised and a lorry stood by to assist with transport. Hopes began to fade on the 18th with no sign of the Mosquitos at midday. By the following morning it would be too late.

Warmly clad against the cold and always on the move to avoid rousing any suspicion, the dedicated band of Underground workers scanned the wintry sky in the direction of Albert. At precisely one minute past twelve o'clock, small black dots started to appear in the sky, flying very low. Despite the appalling conditions for take-off at Hunsdon, the climb through snow-filled cloud, and being unable to see the ground from 500 feet over England, the first Mosquitos swept into the attack one minute behind schedule.

Three of the aircraft from 487 Squadron went straight to the target to drop their eleven-second delay bombs. The remaining two made a feint on the railway station at Amiens to create the diversion, the third aircraft in this flight with Tich Hanafin having returned with engine trouble to England. The eleven second delay bombs were a necessity to allow the aircraft to be well clear of the target before the bombs exploded.

464 Squadron was hard on the heels of 487, too close in fact for safety, as the first bombs had not exploded. Wing Commander Bob Iredale was leading this squadron in which Charles Pickard was to be the last to bomb before assessing the damage and he quickly realised that a straight run-up to the target was out of the question. Breaking left they completed a 360-degree turn during which they passed over Glisy Airfield to the accompaniment of flak from the defending guns. The debris thrown up by the first wave had scarcely settled when 464 Squadron bore down on the prison. Inside the prison, hell had already started.

The author is indebted to Monsieur Henri Moisan, one of the loyal French who had been incarcerated in the prison, for his very personal account of events after the first bombs fell.

'Lunch, in the form of a plate of watery soup was about to be served. The nearby church tower had just finished striking twelve o'clock.

'Planes passing over delighted us. At this time the Allies had the mastery of the air. The squadrons which flew past were rarely troubled by German fighters and they were nearly always out of range of the anti-aircraft guns. The bombers flew high, almost always invisible at the extreme end of their long silver vapour trails.

'It was always a spectacular sight, full of excitement, and on this we feasted our eyes, and our hatred, every day. Those beautiful silver stoles criss-crossing the skies represented for us the glaring signs of the enemy's suffering and of his defeat. Were they not also the signs of our own liberation? Our minds used to imagine a bombardment made-to-order, one which would break down the walls of the prison and burst open our cells, without of course, killing anyone inside except the German guards! And now, on the 18th February, 1944, although fantastic and quite beyond our belief, but nonetheless real, we received our made-to-measure bombardment. Unfortunately it was not to be without casualties.

'Noon. The fatigue men begin to dish out the soup. As I wait for the so-called soup, I am reading. Suddenly I hear the noise of powerful engines approaching. It is an aircraft, painted a dull khaki with tri-colour markings, flying over at roof-top height. A violent explosion shatters our window panes. Frightened, we step back towards our cell door. Explosions follow, one after the other in quick succession. I suddenly feel myself going down with the debris as the building disintegrates in a mass of bricks, concrete and beams. I find myself a few metres lower down, buried under the rubble, dazed and stunned, but without quite losing consciousness.

'I am boxed in, squeezed on all sides, and bruised. I feel incapable of any movement. I choke and am unable to breathe properly because of the crushing weight on my chest. I do not know if I am wounded. My mind is in a daze. The bombing goes on and I feel lost. I commend my soul and the care of those I love to *the one who is out of reach of the bombs*.

'How long does it take to die of suffocation? Thinking of this, I notice that my stone corset so to speak, has loosened a little. I can breathe, feebly but sufficiently. I can hear my name being called by one of my cell mates. I shout and let him know that I am alive. He encourages me, saying that I will be pulled out and I gather that he is not entombed. Later I was to learn that I was the only occupant of the cell to go down with the debris.

'The bombs are still falling and my comrade disappears. What is going on? What is it all about? The landings perhaps? It was a long time afterwards before I knew the answers to these questions.

'After what seemed an eternity, but could only have been a few minutes, the bombing stops at last. From the debris I can hear the sinister chorus of groans. All those buried who are still conscious are crying out, either through pain or to attract a rescue team. Some time passes but I have no idea how long. I ration my shouts to conserve my breath. Suddenly I notice a light, I hear voices becoming more distinct gradually, and at last I understand. They are my rescuers. My shouts have attracted them and one of my fingers sticking out of the debris has guided them. Where is the body at the end of the finger? Whilst falling, my arm became stuck up vertically, thus badly indicating my position.

'Taking great care to prevent a further cave-in, the rubble is removed, my head is freed, and then my body. My legs are pinned under the ceiling, a mass of concrete which, but for a miracle, should have smashed my limbs. I am freed at last, and among my rescuers I recognise one of my prisoner friends, Louis Sellier. He could well have escaped during the ten or fifteen minutes it took the Germans to throw a cordon around what was left of the prison. He had waited at all cost to help in my rescue. For his trouble and his loyalty he was later deported to Germany. Praise be to God, he came back.

'I am laid on a stretcher, still a bit groggy but nevertheless conscious. I am given an injection and something to drink. I try to move carefully. I am delighted that nothing seems to be fractured, only superficial injuries to the face, head and hands, making for a very bloody picture. With an eight day beard, the dust covering my body and my clothing in shreds, I looked like a dying man. I meant to keep it that way. Stiff on my stretcher with my eyes half closed, the Germans took one look at me, and lost interest. They only enquired where I was being taken.

'The Passive Defence people, both men and women, were on the scene before the Germans arrived with ambulances. They succeeded in helping a few of the injured survivors to escape. It is too late for me. In any case I am in no fit state to walk. I am lifted up into an ambulance. The nurse who has taken me in charge, instead of taking me to hospital, takes me to Dr Filachet. She tells the Gestapo that the hospital is full and has no more room. Dr Filachet is my brother-in-law.

'This was my salvation. I expect to be re-captured by the Gestapo at any moment, but during the following weeks such alarming bulletins are issued about my health that the Gestapo decide to give me up as a bad job. To help them in this decision, the bombing of the prison has given the administration authorities enough headaches as they try to identify the victims and search for the escapees. I am more or less forgotten. The arrival of the tanks of the 23rd British Hussars on 31st August liberated me completely.

'As it can be imagined, 18th February was a terrible day for my wife and close relatives. As soon as I was freed from the debris, I was recognised by one of our friends who was a member of the Passive Defence. He hurried to telephone my wife to re-assure her. My wife had heard the explosions but without knowing where they had taken place. She thought that our friend wanted to prepare her for the bad news on my death. In her distress, she hurried to my brother-in-law only to see me rigid on a stretcher, being carried out of the ambulance. She thought I was dead and went into a stupor, only to regain her senses at my bedside when I was able to re-assure her regarding my condition.

'At the time of the bombing, only my brother-in-law worried. Passing by the prison half an hour after the bombing, he had been able to speak to one of my friends, Dr Mans, who was also a prisoner. Although not injured in any way, Dr Mans would have been able to escape without difficulty but decided to remain on the spot to attend to his comrades. My brother-in-law enquired about my fate from Dr Mans who showed him my collapsed cell and the pile of rubble under which I had been buried. My brother-in-law concluded that I must be dead and hurried to the hospital where he knew that his services would certainly be required. At that moment the wounded were beginning to arrive. While operating, he kept an eye on all arrivals in the hope of seeing me alive or dead. In the end, a messenger sent by my sister-in-law gave him my news.

'This was my day on 18th February 1944.'

Henri Moisan survived the war and flourishes to-day as Maitre d'Hotel at an hotel in Amiens. Dr Mans was his friend and knew the family well. The story of Dr Mans remains in the annals of the

Amiens prison raid as one of its greatest heroes.

Dr Antonin Mans was resident in Amiens in May of 1940 when the enemy advance guard were about to enter the town. He was the Public Health Officer and circumstances at that time forced him to become Defence Chief of the Somme area, in addition to his professional duties. The country north of the river Somme was declared a forbidden zone by the Germans and trespassers were prosecuted, on the spot, with a gun. The line of demarcation ran through Amiens and the Germans patrolled the forbidden zone with some vigour. A good part of Amiens lay in ruins after three days of a non-stop barrage from German shells before the enemy entered the town. The town of Abbeville was in no better case with half the city in ruins. The 'scorched earth' policy of the German army had left most of the towns and villages in Northern France a carbon copy replica of the massive damage created in the 1914–18 war. Two hundred and fifty thousand buildings in Dr Mans' department alone had been either flattened or badly damaged. The first years of the war brought a promise of nothing but hardship to the French in the northern sector. Among the ruins and the barbed wire lay the debris of a vanquished French army. The Maginot line, much vaunted though it had been, was but a myth of the past at a stroke. The full might of the German army had proved invincible as in the other countries under Nazi domination. The outlook was bleak.

Dr Mans was allowed to visit prisons on his rounds and he lost no time in making plans as head of Passive Resistance to help some of the prisoners to escape. It was a desperately dangerous game, but to the doctor, necessity knew no laws. On 12th November 1943, Dr Mans was picked up at his home by the Gestapo and sent to be a guest of the Gestapo in Amiens Prison. He was among friends who did not find him wanting in time of need.

The attack by the Mosquitos lasted no more than five minutes. The chaos of bombs exploding, walls collapsing and cell doors being wrenched open was beyond description. It was followed by an uncanny silence in the cold February air. Two of the outer walls had been breached as planned, and before the dust had settled over the prison, the fortunate ones had gathered their wits and were making all speed towards the newly provided exits. One of these was Dr Mans.

Choking with smoke from the fires and covered in dust from the falling building, Dr Mans made his way over the heaps of rubble. The pitiful cries from the trapped, the injured and the dying tore at his heart strings. Without a further thought for himself or his own safety he abandoned all thought of escape. The cries from those he heard were in need of a doctor immediately and Dr Mans was on the spot. If he had any lingering doubts, the sight of a woman lying on the ground with her legs severed quickly removed them. From somewhere above, he heard his name being called by his friend Captain Tempez. Tempez was still locked in his cell but Dr Mans was able to release him quickly from the bunch of keys he had picked up as he made his way through the German guards' quarters which was choc-a-bloc with the dead and the dying guards. Their quarters had received a direct hit.

Captain Tempez quickly asked Dr Mans what he intended to do.

'Stay', replied Dr Mans.

'Very well, I'm with you', answered Captain Tempez, and together they set about the injured around them, French and German alike.

Other prisoners joined them voluntarily, amongst whom was a prisoner called Lenglet. Lenglet himself was injured and had been arrested during a parachute operation. If caught again, he had no chance of survival. He elected to remain behind and help Dr Mans and Captain Tempez. There were others of the same mind and in the same case as Lenglet. Couq, Leboeuf, Clement, Guelton, Lietard. Terreux, amd others. . . . Of these men, no finer example of 'laying down his life for his friends' could be found.

The injured Lenglet, although badly hurt, refused treatment for himself, saying that he would manage well enough as he was. Some of the injured men remained trapped among the wreckage with only a call for help to indicate that a pile of rubble still held a prisoner. One of these was Monsieur Bellemere who had been a solicitor in Amiens and he lay in the worst possible position. He had been confined to a cellar in the building which had collapsed under an enormous pile of debris. While Dr Mans administered to the injured on a hastily provided table, some of the others dug deep into the rubble covering Monsieur Bellemere. They dug from three o'clock in the afternoon, through the night and until one o'clock the following morning. This gallant action was in vain. Monsieur Bellemere died from his injuries one week later.

The blast from the bombs dropped by the Mosquitos against the building with pinpoint accuracy had one unfortunate result. One of the bombs detonated a room full of hand grenades. The grenades in the room had been moved into the prison only the previous week as a further precaution by the Germans against unrest. The additional blast from this room had not been anticipated and it created havoc.

Soup was being served by two young Belgians under the watchful eye and strict supervision of a hard-line German called Otto. Otto was a First World War veteran, loud mouthed, brutal and calculatingly cruel. His manners were in need of repair. This trio of waiters and supervisor had been serving the upper gallery when the main building was struck. By the strangest of fortune, the two young Belgians were thrown to the ground unhurt. Otto landed up on the floor in oblivion.

The patrol on the outside of the prison had been caught by the guns of a Mosquito. Out of the patrol only one survived and he was running round the inside of the prison now, threatening everyone in sight with his sten gun. Blood was pouring from his head as he stood over Dr Mans and his assistants beside the impromptu operating table. The little group worked quietly and quickly, ignoring the German head-case who was still on his feet. Enraged that a soldier of the Third Reich should be ignored in favour of the decadent French prisoners, the head-case raised his gun menacingly. Dr Mans took the man seriously at this stage and decided to calm the animal. He told him to lie on the table and his injury would be inspected at once. It would be a manifest boost to the German's ego if he were advised that his injury was really serious and that the doctor could not understand such inordinate strength to withstand so grievous an injury. Dr Mans boosted his ego, swathed his head in bandages to such an extent that it was impossible for the offensive German to see the light of day, and had him led away to where he could do no harm. He sat quietly in a corner of the yard conveniently blinded, yet reflecting on his inordinate strength.

The diversion caused by the two Mosquitos heading over Amiens in the direction of the prison paid off. It seemed the obvious target and the Mosquitos wasted no time in the target area proper. When the sound of dropping bombs reached the people in the town, and the sound of the engines faded away, all within a matter of minutes, everyone rushed towards the station. No bombs. No devastation. Where had they gone? A pall of smoke spiralled from the direction of the prison, the only tell-tale mark in an otherwise white horizon. Very few realised that hundreds of men and women were, at that moment, making their escape through the blasted walls. Those in the know said nothing, but saw everything. It was almost two hours later before the Germans appeared. Towards two o'clock the confused German soldiery arrived. Their arrival was not hastened by the people of Amiens. They spent a great deal of time looking for unexploded time-bombs in the vicinity of the railway station. By the time the secret was out, the aircraft were back in England.

Dr Mans continued to give help to the injured, without a thought for himself or his future. Four very badly wounded Germans had been found among the carnage of the guardroom. He went at once to tend them. The soldiers did not require a doctor. They were in need of the last rites. Even as he examined them, they died.

With the Germans came the Passive Defence teams. Among them a lady doctor by the name of Odile Regnault of the Public Health Service who took in the extensive damage at a glance and made a fairly accurate report to the authorities later. She was full of admiration for the accuracy of the bombing, particularly to the left wing of the prison where the German guards had been quartered. It had been entirely demolished by a direct hit, practically wiping out the entire guardroom. Those still alive had been so badly injured that there was little hope for their survival. The entire building stood without a roof and only a broken shell of the original building remained. As this was the main nerve centre of the German guards, the work done by the Mosquito bombs had eliminated the guards and facilitated the escape of the prisoners. It was a classic piece of destruction.

The same part of the prison lay open to the outside world where the prison wall had been. Through the huge gap, the cells could be seen with the doors ripped apart, fallen masonry everywhere, with cries from those who had been injured and entombed still coming from the debris.

The outer prison wall had been breached and this had been the main escape exit for the prisoners, allowing them to make for the snow covered fields beyond.

Dr Odile Regnault joined Dr Mans at his crude operating table and together they set-to with a will and with the haste imposed upon them by the steadily mounting stream of wounded. Captain Tempez and his men returned time and time again to the debris to help free the prisoners and carry them to the operating table. The German troops arrived, and with them members of the dreaded Gestapo, in the hope that they could find a lead among the remaining prisoners on other members of the Resistance. Those remaining in the prison were either very badly injured or helping Dr Mans at his table. Dr Mans was quick to realise the purpose for which the Gestapo had accompanied the troops. He warned his helpers and his colleagues to exercise caution. Shortly after, he was taken away by the soldiers and the little band of dedicated men were marched out of the prison gates. They were taken to the old cavalry quarters, to a room on the first floor where straw palliasses had already been laid out. Food was provided by the Red Cross, the first decent soup they had tasted in months.

Braumann, chief of the Gestapo in Amiens arrived with the German troops, accompanied by his interpreter, Lucienne. The Gestapo ignored the plight and the cries of the injured and those entombed as they quickly tried to identify the dead and the dying, going to the extent of taking finger prints of the dead. Braumann commented with admiration on the work carried out by Dr Mans and his helpers and assured the authorities that recognition would be forthcoming from the German authorities. The 'recognition' meted out by the Gestapo for the selfless behaviour of Dr Mans and his helpers was not long in forthcoming. Dr Mans was sent to a labour camp at Fallersleven which was one step short of Buchenwald. He survived the terrible winter of 1944/1945 before being shipped out in cattle trucks on 1st May bound for the Baltic. Many of his fellow prisoners died before they reached the cattle trucks.

En route to the Baltic, the final battle for Europe raged on all sides. Two Allied aircraft destroyed the engine of the train with gunfire. The SS guards accompanying the prisoners made ready to annihilate the entire trainload with machine guns and flame throwers. Other Allied aircraft swept low over the train, threw the

SS into a panic and they fled smartly, leaving the prisoners to their own devices. The following day, the 2nd May, the first American troops arrived. As they did so, a young man of twenty lay dying in the arms of Dr Mans. He had been a hero in the Aisne Resistance and it was to save the prisoners from such a fate that Operation Jericho had been mounted.

On 23rd October 1944, Arras had been liberated. The aftermath of war required a great deal of clearing up. It had been the same story in 1914–1918. The defence ditches had become overgrown in a tangle of tall grass. One of the jobs being carried out by a labourer during that month was the tedious task of cutting the long grass which seemed to have overgrown everything. It was a slow, thankless and cold task. The labourer worked quietly away, occasionally coming upon some relic or other of the grim struggle from which Arras had now been freed. His scythe cut through the grass and he struck a wooden object. Closer examination revealed it to be a wooden slab on which certain names had been written. Further cutting revealed more wooden slabs, each inscribed with names. The labourer reported his find to the authorities.

The area under grass was examined minutely and in due course two hundred and sixty bodies were exhumed. Identification was still possible in some cases from earlier dental work which had been carried out and recorded in the French army files. Among the two hundred and sixty bodies identified was Captain Tempez and his friends who had stayed behind to help Dr Mans at Amiens. They had been shot in the month of April.

A funeral service was held in Amiens Cathedral for the French victims who had died in the attack on the prison. A row of coffins which had been borne by the young men of the Passive Defence lined an area beside the choir. It was perhaps the biggest and most moving ceremony ever to be held in the ancient cathedral at Amiens. The Red Cross workers formed a guard of honour. The reason for the attack was not then generally known. Monseigneur Martin made a short but moving address, in which he referred to 'this unforeseen and mysterious catastrophe'. The opportunity to despise the Royal Air Force was not lost on the Prefet of Vichy who was a well known collaborator of the Germans. In full dress uniform he attended the ceremony to pay homage to the victims. His wisdom

Picard of Picardy 171

did not match his purpose. He had forgotten that many of the victims had been persecuted enemies of the Third Reich and active members of the French Resistance. To the other mourners in their sorrow, Monsieur le Prefet of Vichy became a marked man. Collaborators are a curious pack of people who have a habit of climbing on the band wagon of the winning side. At the time of Amiens, the German band wagon was creaking at the wheels but this did not disabuse the mind of the Prefet of Vichy. The English, he told his reluctant listners, were happy to turn on their Allies. He was not aware that some of the congregation consisted of men and women in the Underground who were acutely conscious of the entire circumstances. With men like Pepe, he should not trifle.

The nerves and the drama on the ground passed unnoticed by those in the air. Conditions on take-off at Hunsdon and for half the Channel crossing had made the leading New Zealand squadron late on target by a minute. Their bombs were set with an eleven-second delay. Three of the New Zealand squadron went straight to the target at zero feet, pulling up at the last minute to avoid the walls and the prison. They attacked the outer walls as planned and lost no time in clearing off to allow the two Mosquitos which had caused the diversion by flying towards the railway station a clear run in to the target.

464 Australian Squadron, led by Wing Commander Bob Iredale, came in low to the prison as the last two Mosquitos of the New Zealand squadron made their attack. Quickly they broke to the left to make a circuit and allow the delayed action bombs time to go off. On this circuit they had to fly low over an airfield and this gave the enemy his first warning that an air raid was in progress. Men could be seen running for their aircraft on the ground below but the pilots felt confident in their ability to drop their bombs and set course for home before the enemy became airborne. They could only hope that 21 Squadron, RAF, were close behind them and would also be able to get clear before being jumped by enemy fighters. Anti-aircraft guns on the airfield hit two of the Australian squadron but the performance of both machines was not impaired.

The enemy guns on the ground in the vicinity of the prison were now fully alerted and anti-aircraft fire was severe. The Typhoon fighters covering the Mosquitos circled the airfield to take care of any fighters taking off. Only four of the original six Mosquitos in this squadron were left to bomb the prison as two had been unable to make contact in the snow conditions over England and had returned to the nearest airfield in Southern England. Smoke and debris could now be seen high in the air as the four aircraft swept in low to attack the guards quarters and the prison itself. In a flash they were through with bombs away. Wing Commander Bob Iredale and Squadron Leader Dick Sugden re-joined each other on the other side of the prison and immediately set course for home as instructed. They could see no other aircraft but knew that Pickard had stayed behind to make the greatest decision of his life. The responsibility rested with Pick to make the decision of calling in 21 Squadron if the two earlier attacks had been unsuccessful.

As Pickard circled at 500 feet over the prison he could see the ant-like figures streaming out and making for the fields in the direction of Amiens. The ground was covered in snow and this made the running figures easier to pick out. Below Mosquito 'F for Freddie' flew the Mosquito of Flight Lieutenant Tony Wickham. In the nose of this aircraft, Lee Howard of the Film Production Unit held his camera at the ready and began taking a film of the damage done to the prison. Howard was apparently oblivious of the danger as he asked his pilot to circle the prison three or four times. Tony Wickham carried out his requests but was less keen to stay in the target area. Neither of them heard the voice of Pickard call out, loud and clear . . . 'Red, red, red. The oranges are ripe'.

21 Squadron breathed a quick sigh of relief and turned about for home. The words were to be the last spoken by Pick to the outside world.

With the mission completed, Pickard turned to make for base. Close by he saw an aircraft lose height and make for the ground, but obviously still under control. He turned immediately to go and check for himself whether any of the crew might escape. Inside the doomed aircraft. Flight Lieutenant R W Sampson was already dead and the pilot, Squadron Leader McRitchie, made a miraculous landing at well over two hundred miles an hour to be thrown clear, survive, and become a prisoner-of-war. Sampson was navigating and had been killed outright by the anti-aircraft fire from the ground. An elderly New Zealander, Sampson and his brother left a widowed mother behind on a farm in New Zealand to join the Royal Air Force. Both were killed.

For the final moments of the Mosquito 'F for Freddie', Group Captain Pickard and Flight Lieutenant Alan Broadley, it has been the author's singular good fortune, amounting to almost a miracle, to be able to trace and make contact with the young French girl of the time, Giselle Cage, who was at the scene of the crash and who tried in vain to help. Her graphic and tragic letter speaks for itself.

As you have asked me I will tell you what happened on that day.

On 18th February we heard the bombs falling near Amiens, the noise of the aeroplanes and a great pall of black smoke rose between Molliens and St Gratien; about a kilometre from our house. We ran full speed in the hope that we might be of some help. Alas! Nothing could be done.

My husband, who was my fiancé at that stage, was in another direction in the fields and saw the aerial battle.

The sky was whitish as it had been snowing. He saw the Mosquito coming from the direction of Amiens flying at about 300 metres, followed at approximately 800 metres by a German fighter. The Mosquito banked to the left. Perhaps he had not seen the German. He then received a shell which cut off his tail which fell spinning to the ground as he turned. The aeroplane then flipped over on its back and dived sharply earthwards.

A hundred metres further on there was a wood and perhaps the aeroplane would not have caught fire if it had fallen in the trees. My husband took his bicycle and went to the scene of the accident.

My father and I were among the first ten people to reach the scene. The aeroplane was burning, or more correctly the engines were burning, as the Mosquito was made of wood and it had shattered on impact and all the pieces were scattered far and wide as well as a certain number of objects ... maps ... camera ... parachutes.

My father gathered up the maps and, after looking at them, he threw them into the fire for we were expecting, at any moment, the arrival of the Germans and he had decided that they must not find any papers. My husband saw another person find a box with

French money in it and it was given to the Mayor of St. Gratien.

Through the smoke we could see two dark shapes between the engines. We thought they must be the airmen. With long sticks cut from the wood the men pushed and pulled. It was extremely dangerous as the heat was making the bullets explode and go off in all directions.

At last they were able to bring the bodies out of the fire and they laid them out on struts of wood from the aeroplane.

I went and retrieved their parachutes and wrapped them in them myself. Captain Pickard still had some scraps of clothing and I cut the wings and ribbons from his jacket to make it more difficult for the bodies to be identified by the Germans. The clothes of Lieutenant Broadley had been completely burned. They were just ashes when he was pulled from the fire.

The bodies had not been burned, just a little swollen from the heat, and the wounds had no blood showing at all. Their faces were black from the smoke. I have never seen photographs of Captain Pickard or Lieutenant Broadley, but I certainly remember their faces well.

We are certain that the two men had been killed by shock on impact. They had remained in a sitting position and one of them had his two arms raised and his hands half clenched. He must have been holding the two handles in the cockpit, no doubt. Perhaps in order to spread or allay the shock.

The aeroplane was low over the wood when it flipped and they struck the ground at once.

The bodies were taken to the Mayor's house at St. Gratien and guarded by the French for as long as possible. The rest is official; you know it. All this is a time in our lives which we will never forget.

I would like to add that, thanks to the intervention and, alas, the sacrifice of Captain Pickard and Lieutenant Broadley, many of our Resistance friends who would have died during the following days were saved. We will always remember them.

Inside the prison, our close friend Doctor Beaumont was killed by a falling beam while trying to escape.

One year later a cross was erected where the aeroplane came to rest, and it was inaugurated.

Another of those quickly on the scene was Monsieur Laurent

Cagnart, the present Mayor of St Gratien village. Among the scattered wreckage he noticed the camera from the aircraft with part of the film torn out and lying in the snow. With most of the others he was an old soldier in the 1914–1918 war and currently active in the Resistance movement. His presence of mind was commendable. Gathering up the camera and the film he hastened to the nearby wood, the Bois Donchel, and found himself a rabbit burrow. Into the burrow he thrust the camera and the film covering the opening with snow as a precautionary measure. He waited long enough, keeping the secret hiding place to himself, until the German soldiery had completed their investigations and left the scene. He then retrieved the camera and film. It was always a possibility that the homes in St Gratien might be searched by the Germans in an effort to ascertain the names of those involved in removing incriminating evidence from the scene of the crash. The village of St Gratien boasted no more than 230 inhabitants. Laurent Cagnart did not receive a visitation, and on 28th November 1944 he handed over the camera and its contents to a British army officer, who issued Monsieur Laurent Cagnart with a receipt.

It read: 'Received from Lawrence Firmin Cagnart, parts of camera and film recovered from Mosquito plane which crashed near St Gratien on 18th February, 1944'.

The receipt was signed by A. Gray, Lieutenant 316169, 226 C.A. Debt., B.L.A. The rabbit burrow and the home of Laurent Cagnart had successfully kept their secret.

At the time the cross was being raised and inaugurated at Amiens, Giselle Cage wrote a very sincere and touching letter to Dorothy Pickard in England. The letter was posted from Molliens-au-Bois in February of 1945. The Allied forces had successfully invaded the Continent, France was being liberated and the Cage family had met a British soldier who had known Alan Broadley well. From this contact, and after a great deal of trouble, Giselle Cage was able to ascertain the address of Dorothy in England. Apart from the letter, the enclosures were astonishing.

The ordinary blue envelope, bursting at the seams, contained Pick's RAF wings and his line of decorations. At the time, Dorothy acknowledged the letter and the gesture with a reply of gratitude. Due to the turmoil of the time, this letter never arrived. It took all of thirty years for Giselle Cage to know that her precious packet had been delivered, and appreciated.

From the original nineteen aircraft which had left Hunsdon in the morning of 18th February 1944, only two returned at the estimated time of arrival. The Mosquitos of Bob Iredale and Dick Sugden were the first to land. The crews of both aircraft made their way to the mess for a late lunch. During the cold and bleak afternoon the other Mosquitos began to arrive in dribs and drabs. For a long time it was impossible to account for all the aircraft. The last flew in from other airfields to which they had diverted because of the weather. In the growing gloom and premature darkness of a bitter February evening, two aircraft remained for which no-one could account by the end of the day. They were the Mosquitos of McRitchie and Pickard. A deep sense of shock suppressed any feeling of accomplishment in the mess. The loss of Squadron Leader McRitchie and his navigator, Flight Lieutenant Sampson, was bad enough. It seemed inconceivable somehow that the great and bustling spirit of Charles Pickard, followed by his inseparable navigator, Alan Broadley, would not suddenly burst through the door and observe to no-one in particular, 'there is always a bloody something!'

The feeling running through the entire mess was summed up by Dick Sugden.

'We waited until late at night, but there was no news. It was unbelievable, but there it was.'

The apprehension was to continue throughout 161 Wing, the Royal Air Force, and Britain for some considerable time.

As late as mid April, hope for the inseparable pair was still being held out. The British press carried banner headlines reading, 'They're Still Together'. Rex North of the *Sunday Pictorial* of 16th April paid a fitting and still hopeful tribute to these two men.

I shall not call it exceptional courage and drown these two men in heroic words because they wouldn't like it. Rather shall I say that if you know a man in the RAF with wings on his chest then you already know a lot about Group Captain Percy Pickard and Flight Lieutenant Alan Broadley.

They were friends, inseparable friends. In 1940 they were in the

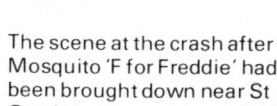

The scene at the crash after Mosquito 'F for Freddie' had been brought down near St Gratien.

The bodies of Pickard and F/Lt. J. A. Broadley being carried through the wood near St Gratien.

The path followed by Mosquito 'F for Freddie' from Amiens prison before being brought down. *(By courtesy of Giselle Souhait).*

The cross on Pickard's grave showing the VC 'awarded' by the magnanimous French, which Dorothy Pickard was asked by the British authorities to have removed.

LAC Albert Sullivan helps Marie Yvonne of Amiens to arrange flowers on Pickard's grave in Saint-Pierre cemetery, Amiens.

Thirty years after: the annual pilgrimage from Amiens prison to the graves of Charles Pickard and Alan Broadley, February 1974. Dorothy Pickard and one of the survivors from the Amiens raid are in front, on the right.

same bomber, flew more than 100 sorties over Europe together, and now they are missing. If you ask a pilot what it is like to sit there while all Hell is breaking loose just below, he probably won't tell you much. But ask yourself what it must be like to do it 100 times, and it would seem that only supermen are capable of standing up to such intense nerve strain.

Pickard and Broadley weren't supermen – at least, no-one who knows them intimately ever dreamed of calling them that. I am sure they didn't feel supermen. They just did a job, did that job well, and were content to carry on doing it. It might have been helpful that neither of them paid the slightest attention to what they would do after the war. They lived for the moment – particularly the moments when they were in the air.

You probably saw Pickard and Broadley in *Target for To-night*. Pick – we'll call him this from now on because it is the name he likes best – was the pilot of 'F for Freddie'. Broadley, quiet, very Yorkshire, was his navigator. In the film they brought their plane, crippled, shot up, thoroughly mauled, back to base . . . but that was fiction. Yet now, in real life, Pick's wife, Dorothy, is sure that her tall, somewhat erratic 28 year old husband will come back again. And in the Yorkshire town of Richmond, that seems to squat on top of a spiral staircase of roads, the proprietor of a small hotel is equally sure that his lad, Alan, will come back with him. He feels that at 22 his son has seen so little of normal life.

If a man becomes a brilliant scientist or mathematician his schoolmaster will always tell you that the genius was brilliant from childhood. Was Pick brilliant? I asked Mr W H Whitworth who was his headmaster at Framlingham College what he was like.

'A nice lad,' he told me, 'but a great problem because he was always bottom of the form. In fact, I didn't know what to do with him when he was ready to leave!'

Mr Whitworth was spared the bother. Pick and a friend hitch-hiked their way, more or less, to Nairobi, bought a truck for £50 and drove back to Piccadilly Circus. Why? 'Just for fun'.

Broadley was much the same. His father won't have it that he was bottom of the form at Richmond Grammar School, but admits that he was always perilously close. When Alan's time came to leave he had no idea what to do with himself either. But at about the same time war was declared, and the problem was solved to Alan's complete satisfaction. He joined the Royal Air Force.

These, then, were the two who met in a bomber. Two men who asked little more from life than a plane, a convenient sky, and a chance to shoot their enemies out of both. Life was dangerous. Life might end any night. Here was adventure.

They dropped leaflets over enemy territory. They bombed enemy towns and military objectives. They flew paratroops to Bruneval. They laughed and joked together while the windows of their plane were being hit by flak and searchlights from nearly every main objective in Europe. Pick collected a DSO and two bars and a DFC. Broadley went to the Palace to collect a DFM, DFC and then a DSO. Brave men? Obviously, yes. Fearless? Obviously, no. Pick, for instance, was once stationed in an old house where the floorboards had parted company with the walls, and it was overrun with rats. Pick put his bed in the middle of the floor, kept the light on – and sat up all night.

Tight corners? Of course there were. There was that time when the plane just wouldn't make the base and they came down in the sea. From his pocket, when they were sitting in a dinghy being buffeted and tossed around, Pick produced a compass the size of a shilling.

'It's all yours Alan', said Pick and tossed the compass to the navigator. For fourteen hours they were in the dinghy with Alan directing. Yes, they were saved. Alan got a DFC for that. And so it went on . . . operation after operation, risk after risk.

At last the Air Ministry decided these two friends had laughed at fate for long enough. They were grounded. Pick was given command of a crack bombing station and he took Alan with him as Officer-in-Charge of Navigation. If Alan had been a careerist he would not have gone, because promotion would have been quicker elsewhere. To stay with Pick meant always being below him in rank. At this point their lives were almost normal. Alan half got himself engaged to a local girl in Richmond, Yorks, while Pick saw his wife and baby. They should have been happy.

In the American Air Force, as you know, a pilot is considered to have done his duty when he has completed a certain number of operations. The limit in the Royal Air Force is slightly more. By this time Pick and Alan had completed the tremendous total of sixty, and had no reason to fly again if they felt that way about it. They didn't feel that way.

'How about an odd operation or two?' they asked.

More thoughts in the briefing room wondering how tough a particular operation was likely to prove, you would suppose; and occasional moments when they asked themselves how long they could avoid misfortune. After all, so many of their friends had come and gone. When was their turn? Apparently they thought nothing of the sort. They thought, instead, of new and better operations, and by better it seems they meant more dangerous.

By this time they had completed over a hundred operations. The Air Ministry sent an artist down to paint them. They were not impressed.

In the early days of 1940, when these two first flew together, Pick had an idea. A crazy idea, perhaps; on the other hand he was rather a superstitious sort of fellow. He blooded Alan in the arm with a needle. Just that.

'That', he said, laughing boyishly, 'makes us blood brothers'.

They will hate this praise, of course, but it is a fact that they are now blood brothers in air glory.

There have been VC's won in this war in the air for brilliant individual feats. These men, too, deserve a VC for going on and on, on a hundred times. And there is still a chance – still a fine, fighting chance – that we shall honour the men themselves, not their memory.

After all, what an extraordinary trick of fate this is. Two friends who were afraid of being parted in the air are missing at the same time. They are in Europe together. Yes, together even if miles apart. Together in a dream to get back to fight again. And, if they do not come back, let us take consolation from the fact that they are together in spirit.

Rex North caught the spirit of the time, the hopes and the fears. Two months after the event, people were still hoping.

The sentiments expressed by Giselle Souhait at the time of the raid were not reflected in the report which appeared in the newspaper of Amiens, *Le Progres de la Somme*. On 19th February, the day following the raid, a full report was made on the front page of *Le Progres de la Somme*. The purpose of the raid had obviously been a well kept secret, and one suspects that the article was written either by a collaborator of the Germans or at the insistence of the German propaganda authorities with a view to profit.

Headed, 'What Happens When The English Come As "Liberators" ', the article ran a banner headline:

'Bombing Of Amiens Prison Causes 40 Deaths And 90 Injured'.

The death toll increases in proportion to the progress made in the difficult task of clearing up. One becomes lost in speculation at the significance of the bloody attack undertaken by the English Air Force yesterday at noon, taking as their objective the prison on Albert Street.

It is no secret that, in addition to the prisoners being held under common law in the prison, there were detainees whose activities had placed them at variance with the occupying forces.

Ever since, the question is being asked (since it has been clearly and irrefutably established that the prison was indeed the target assigned to the pilots) what secret motive prompted this order? If it is a question of 'mass liberation' the many bodies which lie bleeding, torn to bits, and crushed under the rubble stand tragic testimony to the complete success of this shameful undertaking.

The English Air Force – the aircraft flew so low that their markings were clearly visible – attacked Amiens on Friday a few minutes after 12 noon. It already appears certain that their target was deliberately chosen; the prison in Albert Street.

Low cloud allowed the enemy pilots to come in low as they approached the target and they immediately homed in on the buildings, dropping their bombs. It is only by wandering through the outer enclosure that one can grasp the reality of this type of concentrated attack which caused such extensive damage.

A count of the dead and injured was quickly taken. Amiens Prison held several hundred prisoners. Of this number one must deduct the teams of outside workers who had not returned to the prison for lunch in order to arrive at a final tally of victims. One should add to this number those who found themselves free by force of circumstance and who fled either into the fields or towards the town. Others were recaptured in the enclosure itself.

By four o'clock in the afternoon, a hundred or so injured had been evacuated and fifteen dead taken out of the rubble. Unfortunately there were others, many others.

In one spot were two bodies, horribly mutilated, lying in a cell crushed under the weight of cement blocks and bricks, and in another spot people were trying desperately to free other victims, one of whom could be heard.

Everywhere people were probing the mounds of rubble and excavations with every possible speed.

Within a relatively short space of time the French and German authorities, all emergency bodies, medical and ambulance services, the fire department and the police, were on the spot where a large crowd had already gathered, and amongst that crowd the parents of detainees at whose anguish one can only guess.

One cannot but make mention of the fact that one bomb fell on one of the outside wards of Hospice St. Victor Hospital where there are two injured. Others fell on many dwelling places around the prison. Two houses were completely destroyed. Showers of shrapnel fell in the neighbourhood but there were no casualties. The clearing up operations carried on through the night by the light of the Home Guard's searchlights. Need I harp on the unstinting effort and courage of the rescue teams who strived to drag the living from the arms of death?

On the Saturday morning the provisional toll at ten o'clock read as follows: 'About forty dead, some of the injured having died in Nouvel Hospital, and about a hundred injured'.

More bodies are continually being discovered in proportion to the progress being made in these difficult operations.

The complete absence of identity papers makes identification of the victims difficult in the extreme. Four of the wounded died in Nouvel Hospital where they had been taken.

During the aerial attack on Amiens, Madame Jeannot, wife of the Divisional Commissioner of Police, was injured in the right arm by a small machine-gun shell. The victim was in her kitchen. She was struck by the bullet which came right through the lounge and the dining room. Dr. Pauchet who is attending her thinks that amputation can be avoided.

Around 12.20, immediately after the bombing and following aerial combat, two of the enemy aircraft were shot down, one at Poulainville and the ther at St Gratien. Each aircraft had a team of two men. Three of the occupants were killed and the fourth, a pilot, was injured. He is in hospital in the care of the occupation forces.

This report from *Le Progres de la Somme* on the 19th was followed on the 22nd by another.

Under the heading, 'Bombing of Amiens Prison. Rescuers Uncover New Bodies', the report begins:

At the last count 71 dead.

During the whole of Sunday the crowds have continually been flowing to the approaches of the prison where the work of clearing up has been continuing day and night without respite. More bodies have been taken out of the rubble but it is obvious even now that means other than picks and shovels must be used in order to pull from the tangle in blocks of concrete, twisted iron and frames the last victims – several dozen, no doubt, whose bodies, in terribly crushed condition are, in certain places visible in part only; an arm, a leg, a head . . . .

It is this terrible sight which acts as a spur for all those who, for the last three days, have been applying themselves to a task involving unheard of difficulty with an effort which can never be sufficiently commended. Whilst the grizzly task is being carried out, the prison personnel have been endeavouring to salvage everything that can possibly help in the reconstitution of the clerical records.

In reply to the many questions we should mention that during the night of Friday and into Saturday several rounds and surveys were made in order to establish whether some of the survivors might still be buried. No groans or cries could be heard and those who could be saved during these tragic hours were the last.

As and when the bodies were recovered they were taken to a nearby spot where, on Saturday afternoon, the identification procedure was begun, as far as this was possible. It was an extremely difficult task due to the almost complete absence of papers. Only the patient assistance of the warders and the specialist personnel of the police judiciary made possible the identification of some of the pathetic remains.

By the end of Sunday afternoon 62 bodies (of whom 37 were identified) had been taken to the temporary mortuary. To this number must be added nine dead in Nouvel Hospital (of whom six were identified), which brings the death toll to 71.

When we left the ruins of the prison, which was completely destroyed, the team of firemen was working on the task of extracting several bodies lying buried under enormous blocks of masonry. Other groups, with the help of a tractor from Magasins Generaux, were continuing the clearing up of one of the shattered buildings and a huge mound of heavy rubble under which there are sure to be bodies which will not be reached for several days.

Let us add that since the early hours of the morning a kitchen has been operating on the spot serving hot drinks and snacks to the workers.

As and when they were put into their coffins, the bodies were taken to Jean-Mace School as the funerals will take place on Tuesday at the town's expense.

The municipal funerals for the victims of the last aerial attack will take place on Tuesday 22nd February at 10 a.m. in the grounds of the girls' school in Jean-Mace Street.

Any lingering doubts on the loyalties of the French who contributed the article in *Le Progres de la Somme* in February of 1944 were dispelled in the editorial comment by G S Savigny. In the same edition of 22nd February he protests:

A prison is not a military target and, at first sight, one cannot understand the air attack on such a building. One can understand it even less since many of the inmates are on the same side as those who carried out the raid.

The Anglophiles will raise the objection that it was precisely the confusion brought about by the bombing which allowed several detainees, held as Gaullists or Communists, to take to the fields.

If that was the purpose of the exercise it was far from being achieved since most of those who were thus 'set free' were killed during the bombing of the prison. In fact, it was the political section which suffered most to the extent that the great majority of the dead were amongst those whose escape they were trying to effect.

Evidently they were set free in the most tragic manner possible.

It cannot be denied that several prisoners did, nonetheless, escape, but they will not enjoy their new found freedom for long.

It would be stretching the imagination too far to even contemplate that the English or American aircraft took them on board for the purpose of transporting them back to England.

Short of means, they will be unable to travel and most of them, obliged to remain in the vicinity, will be tracked down in the sharpest possible fashion. They will be forced to live from hand to mouth and since amongst them there are not only partisans but also suspect elements, the former will be conspicuous by their thefts, looting, or worse.

Some dead; others condemned to give themselves up before long or to wander around the countryside under fear of recapture, this will be the clear-cut result in this act of liberation by bombing and deliberate destruction.

In the final analysis, the total number of individuals who lost their lives as a direct result of the Amiens raid amounted to 87. Those recaptured amounted to 182, but the Germans could not account for a hefty total of 255 prisoners. Like the wind, they had gone.

Official notification by letter was received on the 24th September. The letter was sent from Air Ministry (Casualty Branch), 73–77 Oxford Street, London, and was addressed to Dorothy at her home in Selsey, Sussex. It read, quite simply,

> Madam,
>
> I am commanded by the Air Council to inform you that they have with great regret to confirm the telegram in which you were notified that your husband, Acting Group Captain Percy Charles Pickard, DSO, DFC, Royal Air Force, lost his life as the result of air operations on 18th February 1944.
>
> After careful personal investigation at Amiens by a senior officer of the Royal Air Force, it has been established that your husband and his navigator were killed at St. Gratien village, eight miles from Amiens, on 18th February, and that they were buried

in St. Pierre Cemetery, Amiens, by the enemy.

The Air Council desire me to express their profound sympathy with you in your bereavement.

I am, Madam,
Your obedient servant,
Signed J. A. Smith.

On Tuesday, 5th December 1944, at 12 noon, a memorial service was held at St Martin-in-the-Fields, London. It was the final tribute to be paid to the inspiring memory of the two men who had elected to become blood brothers at the beginning of their career together, and who had made the supreme sacrifice at Amiens. Over the years, Amiens itself pays a lasting tribute. A service is held annually on the Sunday closest to 18th February in the old cathedral at Amiens to the memory of those who died in the raid. The service finished, the congregation leave the cathedral and march to the cemetery of St Pierre. By the gravesides of Charles Pickard and Alan Broadley, a second simple service is held, and wreaths laid afresh. It is attended by relatives and friends of those who were killed at Amiens and by members of the Royal Air Force from their last squadron. By the noble French whom they died to save, they have not been forgotten.

Prior to the raid on Amiens, Dorothy and Pick had moved to Hunsdon to allow Pick to work up the three squadrons for the coming attack. They felt that it was a temporary measure and their beloved Ming was left at Sculthorpe in charge of Pick's second-in-command. Few feeding instructions were required as rabbit was off-ration and Ming was very fond of rabbit.

The wait for Dorothy at Hunsdon was shared by the entire station. The two aircraft were missing, but there was always the chance that news would filter through, even if the network in the Picardy region had been thrown into an uproar. The afternoon of the 18th sped by into evening. Outside, the snow continued on its dismal way while Dorothy, the Wing, and the high-ups in Air Ministry waited.

The telephone rang. Call for Mrs Dorothy Pickard. Dorothy answered the telephone. Pick's second-in-command from Sculthorpe was on the end of the line.

Without any preamble, Dorothy was asked if she could return at once to Sculthorpe. Ming was very ill and vomiting blood. Dorothy asked whether a vet had been called. She was assured that two vets had examined the dog and there was nothing organically wrong with Ming. Temperature was normal, pulse beats, but appetite nil.

Dorothy was given a staff car from Hunsdon and set off for Sculthorpe, tortured by the thought of Pick's being missing and now Ming being sick. Outside the car it was snowing. She was driven through the darkness to Sculthorpe. Late in the evening they arrived, with Dorothy desolate. She was taken to see Ming immediately.

The dog lay stretched at full length on the floor of the lounge, vomiting blood. With barely a recognition, Ming lay dormant. Dorothy turned to Pick's second-in-command, drained of any more feeling.

'Pick is dead,' she announced.

The words were at once ominous, tragic, and much ahead of their time.

The second-in-command tried his best to comfort and re-assure Dorothy. He was not au fait with Ming, nor of the workings of the mind of an extraordinary dog.

Whatever her hopes had been, in that instant when Dorothy first set eyes on Ming lying on the floor and vomiting blood, she had a feeling of terrible finality. She remembered the odd nights when Ming had awakened her; the ditching in the North Sea, being bogged down in France in the Hudson, and now, this. With the stoicism born of endless trial and tribulation, Dorothy tried to explain her sentiments to the second-in-command at Sculthorpe. He would have none of it, and any animal telepathy was beyond his ken. For months Dorothy kept her own council. By virtue of hand feeding and constant attention, Ming rallied from her stupor although the big dog lay at death's door for a full month.

During the month Dorothy had a visitor. It was Lord Londonderry, apologising for intruding upon her privacy and anguish at this time. There was nothing he could say to allay her grief. With him he carried a letter which he handed to Dorothy. The letter was undated. It read:

Royal Air Force

Dear Lord Londonderry,

I am writing this short letter to you and handing it in a sealed blank envelope to my adjutant, to be opened and delivered to you if I should fail to return from a sortie.

For nearly two years now I have had a feeling that one day or night I shall be knocked down, and although I myself am not afraid, I do feel my responsibilities.

The morning you tried to persuade me to take you on a raid, I decided at that moment, that when my son was born, I should invite you to be his godfather, as I felt confident that you would do all in your power to help and advise Dorothy as to my son's future.

Financially Dorothy is safe, although I have no money my pension plus the small income that Dorothy has will be sufficient to look after them both, anyhow it is my wish that Dorothy should marry again, in which case she will have nothing to worry about.

My other wish is that Nicholas should be educated at my old school 'Framlingham College' or some other similar college, which is not considered expensive. On leaving school at no more than $17\frac{1}{2}$ years, he should be sent abroad for a period of at least three years, with an allowance sufficient only to keep him if that is necessary, no more than £100 per year.

At the end of that period, I should like him to return to this country, and join the Royal Air Force and endeavour to obtain a permanent commission.

Under no circumstances should his hand be forced. If he wishes to remain overseas for good, he may do so, but he is to be given no financial assistance whatsoever and after reaching 21 years of age his allowance shall cease.

I am not informing Dorothy of my intentions regarding Nicholas, but should like you, to communicate with her immediately I am posted missing.

My adjutant has instructions to communicate with you should this occur and he also has instructions to open the sealed envelope and will find this addressed to you.

Should, on the other hand, I be taken prisoner, I would like you to do all you can for Dorothy and the baby, but under no circumstances are you to help financially. Dorothy has instructions regarding this matter.

My chances of being taken alive are remote as I always carry a revolver and intend fighting it out. If you hear I am a prisoner it will be because either I am too badly injured to fight, or because I funked it.

In conclusion, I should like to thank you for what you have done for me, and also to inform you that I have every confidence in you carrying out my instructions.

Finally, I cannot speak too highly of Bomber Command particularly the men who are least mentioned, the wireless ops, and the gunners, their risks are greater than anyone's, yet they are the least rewarded.

Good luck,
Charles Pickard.

The methodical mind of the man who had planned the attacks on so many targets over enemy territory, and led them, was fully apparent in his final letter. The last sentence in which he mentioned the wireless operators and the gunners as those who took the greater risks and were least rewarded was the thinking of a kind, open and generous mind. It was typical of Pick who put his home first, his animals second, and his career third.

Lord Londonderry remained long enough to comfort Dorothy, at the same time assuring her of his unqualified help in any times of need ahead. It was a time when Dorothy was in sore need of support and understanding from her closest friends. For Dorothy, the war finished at Amiens.

The French wanted to bury the two men with every honour but the Germans took over and, on 19th February, both were laid to rest in a cemetery not far from the prison. The Germans, with little respect for the French desire to see their comrades buried, forbade the burial to be attended by anyone. This did not stop the villagers and they attended the graveside to pay their last respects. Later, when Northern France was liberated, members of 140 Wing paid a visit to Amiens and were shown the prison, the wreckage of Mosquito 'F for Freddie', and the graves of the two airmen. The French had made their own rules with which the British authorities did not agree. The cross guarding the grave bore the legend Group Captain P. C. Pickard, VC, DSO, DFC, Bar. They had mixed up the bars but this was a minor issue. In their peculiarly generous and noble way, they had decided to award Pick the VC. As no foreign power is recognised or allowed to award the Victoria Cross, or any other British decoration for that matter, the only diplomatic way to have the VC removed from the headstone was to ask Dorothy to request that the VC be removed. Dorothy complied with the request.

Epilogue

In February of 1944, Dorothy was left with one child of thirteen months, one dog of five years, and a host of memories. The letter which Pick had written to Lord Londonderry was in the nature of Pick's last will and testament. By the end of the war, Ming had recovered sufficiently to produce a litter of bouncing pups. The winter of 1948 in Britain was sufficiently severe to make Dorothy think seriously of the Colonies and remove herself from memories. Her decision was helped by the letter from Pick to Lord Londonderry of which she now had a copy.

Kenya had been Pick's idea of living, but Dorothy decided to move further south. She chose what was then Southern Rhodesia. Accompanied by one small son, Ming and a nine month old daughter of Ming, Dorothy set sail for pastures new. The passage out called at Cape Town and Beira in Portuguese East Africa. Her first introduction to the Africans who came on board to clean the cabin at both ports was one of mystery. None of the cleaning staff would go near her cabin. Ming and her pup, shaggy, big and silent, were considered 'English Lions!'

The hot and humid port of Beira on the east coast of Africa was a far cry from the cold waters of Southampton and neither of the dogs was dressed for the occasion. The heat is intense and the long woolly coats of the dogs made them a mort uncomfortable. Young Nicholas was now six and, like his valiant father, already showed signs of accepting a challenge. The water in the bay at Beira was a welcome change from the icy waters around Britain. He made full use of their short stay in Beira to improve his swimming.

It is a long overnight haul by rail from Beira as the train climbs out of the swampy flats around the town to the highland country of Umtali in Rhodesia. With the altitude, the temperature changes, and by morning the crisp fresh air replaced the almost fetid

Epilogue

temperatures and malarial conditions of East Africa. It was most appreciated by the two English sheep dogs.

In accordance with his father's wishes, Nicholas was sent to a suitable primary school and then to Peterhouse School in Marandellas. Dorothy and the dogs remained in Salisbury, an easy hour's run from the country town of Marandellas. It would be fairly accurate to say that Peterhouse School is an approximate replica of Framlingham. The fees are moderate, the schooling excellent, and discipline strict. During holidays the outdoor life was taught. They slept under trees.

The outdoor and open air life of Africa is conducive to all manner of sport and, growing into manhood, young Nicholas had few thoughts of returning to Britain to seek a commission in a flying capacity with the Royal Air Force. The small and evergreen fields of England with the massive population were no substitute for the sun and the vast spaces of the African continent, and Nick did not return, except to visit his relatives.

Time moved on apace and Ming, at the age of fourteen began to show signs of old age and suffering. She was taken to the vet for a check-up and the report was an ominous one. Her kidneys were not functioning properly. Dorothy was advised to have the old dog quietly put to sleep with an injection. Dorothy would have none of it. How could the vet, any vet, begin to understand? The dog had been given to Dorothy by Pick, a nine month old pup, as a wedding present. Ming had joined them every available morning to follow the two horses as Dorothy and Pick went out on their early morning rides. When rabbits were seen by Pick, he would quickly whistle up the eager sheep dog, with four sharp blasts using his fingers and the dog would race up to leap over the hedge or fence in the direction Pick's arm was pointed. In a flash it would be rabbit for dinner as the dog leapt back over the hedge with a well fed rabbit in her mouth, wagging her tail, awaiting a word of congratulation from her master. This was always forthcoming and Ming positively purred.

Later, war became more serious and time demanding on Pick's early morning rides, but the dog was never happier and never more active than when following the two ex-racehorses from Newmarket across the heath. Cross country flights became a substitute for the regular morning hunts and Ming acquired her own flying log book in which she was given the honorary title of 'Observer'.

Raids over enemy territory, with Ming left behind to fret became a regular and increasing occurrence. It would be difficult for the ordinary vet to understand the occasions when Dorothy was awakened in the middle of the night as Ming pulled the bedclothes from the bed. When Pick had ditched in the North Sea for the worst part of fourteen hours, the uncommonly fearful time when the Hudson became bogged down in France when hope was almost given up of getting the aircraft off the ground, and Amiens. No, it would be too much to ask a vet to try and understand.

Dorothy took the big dog home, determined to nurse the animal as long as her help was needed. It was not easy to manhandle the large helpless Ming out to the garden whenever necessary, and Dorothy used a rug on which she placed Ming, and dragged her along the floor. Ming lingered on without showing any signs of improvement. The old lady had to be fed by hand and dragged gently to the garden for some months. The rainy season of 1951 had started, and with the rains, Christmas and New Year passed as the countryside became everywhere green and lush. Into February the rains continued with Ming becoming less robust, showing little interest and almost in a comatose state, unable to move a muscle.

The quiet in Africa comes shortly before the dawn, with a stillness which can be felt. Dark, massive, brooding Africa.

Dorothy was asleep in her room with Ming lying in the lounge. In the utter darkness Dorothy was awakened by a small plaintive cry from Ming. She arose at once, feeling that the dog wanted to attend the needs of nature and had to be taken out to the garden. Switching on the light in her bedroom, Dorothy threw on her dressing gown, ever alive to the needs of Ming, and made her way to the lounge to help.

With Ming on the carpet, Dorothy began to pull the dog towards the door. The passage of the house was long. Half-way towards the door a loud, clear and four sharp blasts of a whistle assailed Dorothy's ears. It was the whistle that Dorothy remembered Pick had made when calling up Ming to chase the rabbits in the heath at Newmarket in the hectic days. The whistle was so clear and so distinct that Dorothy left Ming for a moment to open the back door of the house to check that it was not an early morning milkman on his rounds. She opened the door to utter darkness, stillness and the African night. Confused, she returned to Ming. The dog lay supine. With that determination born of dedicated women in a time of crisis, Dorothy returned to pull Ming towards the door and the garden.

Ming was taken safely out to the garden and left for a time to her own devices while Dorothy went down to her African compound to find out if any of her servants were awake. The dog was unable to move a limb as Dorothy left her to check on the servants. In the African quarters, Dorothy called out to see if anyone was awake and had anyone whistled. There was no reply. The servants were all sound asleep.

Moving through the grounds, Dorothy kept calling out . . .

'Anyone there . . . anyone there . . . ?'

There was no reply. The first streaks of dawn were scoring the east when Dorothy returned to the house, and Ming. Somehow, in a fashion which Dorothy could not begin to understand, Ming had raised herself on to her haunches, front legs placed firmly on the ground. The dog had been unable to rise for months. As Dorothy looked at Ming, full of compassion, the old dog was raising her head, to the left and to the right, looking upwards towards the early morning sky.

For a moment the hours of torment flooded back. The North Sea. The Hudson. Amiens. Slowly, ever so slowly, Ming continued to raise her head, to the left and to the right. She was very tired and the movement of the old dog's head was obviously causing an effort of which she was scarcely capable. Slowly the movement stopped, the head dropping dejectedly to her chest.

The early morning was still silent, with never a movement from the wind or the trees. Of a sudden, out of the silence came four clear, shrill blasts . . . such as only Pick made with his fingers, so many years ago. Not only did Dorothy hear the shrill blasts; they were heard by Ming. With a supreme effort, the dog raised her head straight towards the sky. The old eyes opened, for a moment she stared at the sky looking straight upwards, and without a sound, Ming dropped to the ground. Dorothy rushed forward to comfort her. The old English sheep dog was beyond all aid. She had gone to chase rabbits with Pick.

Dorothy returned empty handed to the house. She brewed a pot of tea such as she had done in more violent times. She was still sitting on her own in the house when the morning newspaper was delivered. Dorothy opened the paper without interest. It was 19th February 1952.

The years between had not been forgotten. Sixteen miles north of London and five miles south of St Albans, near the village of London Colney, one of England's more stately homes rears its illustrious roof to the sky. The stately home is Salisbury Hall. As historic houses go, it is by no means large, but it must rank among the loveliest. It is set in rolling, undulating parkland and is surrounded by the tall and lovely trees of olde England. Setting off the front and the approach to Salisbury Hall is a protective moat, reminiscent of times mediaeval.

Here had been created and tested the first Mosquito, known as W 4050. She has also been immortalised by being returned to Salisbury Hall and placed in a hangar as the show piece among other relics in the official and only Mosquito Museum in the world.

Thirty years later to the day since the first flight of the Mosquito fighter/bomber was flown by Geoffrey de Havilland Junior, the Liverpool Corporation handed over one of the last Mosquitos ever built to the museum at Salisbury Hall. Among the guests who had been invited to attend was Dorothy Pickard who had made a trip half way across the globe for the occasion. The ceremony was attended by some of the men who had made the de Havilland Mosquito into a legend and some of the dedicated team who worked in secret in 1940 to help create the legend. Among those present to watch Dorothy Pickard unveil the memorial was Colonel Maurice Buckmaster, a wartime head of the French Section of the Special Operations Executive, with whom the Royal Air Force planned the Amiens raid.

Other famous pilots present at Salisbury Hall included Group Captain Leonard Cheshire, VC, and Group Captain (Cat's Eyes) John Cunningham. They were able to meet many of the people who helped to design and build the aircraft, as the Mosquito Appeal Committee had managed to trace eighty of the original Salisbury Hall team.

Epilogue

The Lord Mayor of Liverpool, Councillor Ian Levin, handed over the log books of the final Mosquito to rest at Salisbury Hall to Group Captain Cunningham who is still with the de Havilland Group and is one of the committee of the Mosquito Appeal Fund.

Dorothy Pickard moved forward to unveil the memorial to her gallant husband and Alan Broadley. It was a moment of memories to everyone present. The aircraft had been painted in the colours and with the identification letters of the Mosquito flown by Pick and Broadley to Amiens.

The gift of the aircraft was a magnificent gesture from the City of Liverpool and perpetuates the memory of those who lived through Amiens, and those who died.

As the assembled crowd stood in silence for a moment at the end of the ceremony, one of the last Mosquitos still flying made three low level, high speed passes over the grounds. The aircraft was flown by test pilot Pat Fillingham, one of the test pilots who had helped develop the Mosquito.

The climax was not complete nor the day ended. Pat Fillingham left the small group round Mosquito 'F for Freddie' and set course for the old airfield at Hunsdon from which the raid on Amiens had taken place. Swords had been beaten into ploughshares and RAF Hunsdon stretched below as a flourishing farm. The cement runway could still be seen stretching across the length of the ploughed lands, still with its uncomfortable dip in the centre.

The Mosquito circled the airfield, throttled back, lowered flaps to reduce speed and flew low and slowly along the old runway.

With a feeling of infinite reverence, a wreath was dropped.

Awards

Charles Pickard

Distinguished Flying Cross
London Gazette dated July 30th, 1940.
(No Citation)

Distinguished Service Order
London Gazette dated March 7th, 1941.
(No Citation)

Bar to the DSO
London Gazette dated May 26th, 1942.
Citation:
Acting Wing Commander Percy Charles Pickard, DSO, DFC.

This officer has made his squadron an extremely efficient bombing force. He has extracted the maximum effort from all, at the same time promoting and fostering an excellent comradeship between flying personnel and ground staff, thus instilling the team spirit so necessary to achieve success. He has instituted a fine spirit among his flying crews for accurate bombing and in obtaining photographs.

On 27th February 1942, he led the force of aircraft which carried the parachute troops who made the raid on Bruneval, thus again demonstrating his outstanding powers of leadership and organization, By his courage, self-sacrifice and devotion to duty, this officer has set an example which, although attained by few, is admired by all.

Second Bar to the DSO
London Gazette dated March 26th, 1943.
Citation:
This officer has completed a very large number of operational mis-

sions and achieved much success. By his outstanding leadership, exceptional ability and fine fighting qualities, he has contributed in a large measure to the high standard of morale of the squadron he commands.

Czech Military Cross
(Awarded by Free Czech Government for his services with 311 Squadron.)

Awards

Alan Broadley

Distinguished Flying Medal
London Gazette dated September 23rd, 1941.

Distinguished Flying Cross
London Gazette dated April 20th, 1943.
Citation:
Acting Flight Lieutenant J A Broadley, DFM. No 161 Sqn.

Flt Lt Broadley has flown as navigator since April 1940. He has fulfilled the duties of Squadron Navigation Officer with great success in two operational squadrons. On one occasion the aircraft in which he was flying came down at sea and it was entirely owing to Flt Lt Broadley that the crew were rescued. On two other occasions he has been involved in air accidents, but this officer continues to show an unabated enthusiasm for operational duties.

Distinguished Service Order
London Gazette dated October 19th, 1943.
Citation:
Acting Flight Lieutenant John Alan Broadley, DFC, DFM. (47690), Royal Air Force. 161 Squadron.

Flight Lieutenant Broadley is a navigator of exceptional merit. He has completed a large number of sorties, rendering most valuable service, and his efforts have contributed materially to the successes achieved.

Index

Abbeville 136, 142, 165
Abingdon 61
Aircraft:
  Anson 43, 44, 91
  Audax 28
  Blenheim 86, 87
  Catalina 55
  Deliant 45
  de Soto 87
  Halifax 78, 92, 111, 112, 113, 114
  Harrow, 28
  Hart 28
  Havoc 78
  Heinkel 43, 44
  Hudson 78, 87, 91, 93, 94, 100, 101, 102, 125, 127
  Hurricane 132
  Lysander 77, 78, 79, 83, 84, 85, 87, 91, 92, 106, 107, 108, 110, 111, 114, 115, 118, 119, 120
  Miles Mentor 58
  Mosquito 130, 131, 132, 133, 135, 138, 139, 140, 149, 150, 151, 153, 156, 159, 160, 161, 166, 168, 172, 173, 176, 194
  Oxford 87
  SE 5a 21
  Spitfire 131, 136
  Tiger Moth 25, 57, 58, 87, 131, 132
  Typhoon 156, 159, 160, 172
  Ventura 129, 133
  Wellington 38, 43, 45, 47, 48, 49, 51, 52, 56, 57, 101
  Whitley 58, 61, 64, 65, 69, 78, 82, 83
Aisner, Julienne 118

Albert 148, 156, 161
Amiens Raid 142–189
Angers 120, 126
Angouleme 112
Arles 81, 94, 96, 97
Arras 142, 170
Atlantic, North 53, 55
Avignon 95

Babington-Smith, Constance 136
Baird, Fl. Lt. 136
Baldwin, Air Marshall Sir John 32, 58
Baldwin, Tony 58
Ball, Albert 105
Baltic 137, 169
Bapaume 149
Bardet, Roger 125, 126, 127
Baronski, Group Captain 46
Barrett, N. F. 20
Baseden, Yvonne 124
Bathgate, Flying Officer 111, 114
Bawdsey 113
Beaumont, Dr 174
Beaurin, Jean 144, 145
Beekman, Yolande 123
Beira 190
Belfast 28, 32
Belgium 82
Bellemere, M. 166
Belsen 125
Berger 54
Berlin 49, 50, 96, 123, 136
Betts, Sergeant 113
Bismarck 52, 53, 54, 55, 56
Bleicher, Sergeant 126

Bloch, Denise 124
Blois 94, 95
Boemelburg, Karl 121, 122
Booker, Flying Officer 65
Boulogne 58
Bowen, Squadron Leader 132
Boxer, Wing Commander A. H. C. 77
Braithwaite, Group Captain, F. 53
Bremen 43, 45, 46, 57, 76
Brest 53, 55, 56, 57
Bridger, Flight Lieutenant 85, 86
Brindisi 77
Britain, Battle of 116, 132
Broadley, Flight Lieutenant Alan 37, 38, 39, 40, 41, 42, 43, 57, 58, 133, 134, 152, 157, 172, 173–6, 189, 195
Browning, Major General 64
Bruneval Raid 59–68, 105
Buchenwald 127, 169
Buckingham Palace 71, 102, 135
Buckmaster, Colonel Maurice 120, 194
Budley 32
Burke, Eric 74

Cabourg 83, 90, 99
Cage, Giselle 173–174, 175, 179
Cagnart, Laurent 175
Caithness 53
Caldwell, Warrant Officer 111, 112, 114
Campbell, Flying Officer Kenneth 53
Carlin, Sidney 'Timbertoes' 21, 22, 44, 45, 46, 47
Caskie, Rev Donald 96, 97, 98, 99
Central Africa 23, 24
Chamberlain, Neville 73
Channel Dash 56, 57
Charteris, Lieutenant E. C. B. 63, 65, 66
Chatreau 58
Cherbourg 95
Chertsey 36
Cheshire, Wing Commander Leonard 135, 194
Churchill, Odette 78, 124, 125
Churchill, Winston 37, 57, 73, 74, 124, 140

Coastal Command 54, 55
Cobb, John 29
Cologne 57
Comp, André 137
Coningham, Air Marshal Sir Arthur 148, 152
Cook, Commander F. 61
Cook, Sergeant 65
Cox, Flight Sergeant C. W. H. 61, 62, 63, 65, 66
Cranwell, RAF 32
Craven, Sergeant 65, 113
Cunningham, Group Captain John 194

Dachau 123
Dalton, Hugh 73, 74, 116
Damerment, Madeleine 123
Déricourt, Henri 88, 116–128
Dieppe 139, 159
Dishforth, RAF 69
Donnington 29
Dorsetshire 55
Doullens 156, 159
Dunkirk 98
Dusseldorf 57

East Africa 21, 45
East Wretham 43
Eindhoven 129
Eisenhower, General 141
Elizabeth, Queen 69–71
Embry, Air Chief Marshal Sir Basil 105, 137, 138, 139, 148, 149, 150, 151, 154, 155
Emden 58
Esmonde, Lieutenant Commander Eugene 55
Essen 57
Etretat 58
Everett, Lieutenant Commander W. G. 61

Fallersleven 169
Farley Wing Commander Walter 76
Fecamp 58, 59, 65

Ferguson, Harry 130
Fielder, Wing Commander E. H. 77
Fielding-Johnson, Flight Lieutant 45
Figg, Flying Officer 94, 99, 105
Filachet, Dr 164
Fillingham, Pat 195
Flushing 57
Foster, Pilot Officer 58, 83
Frazer, Henri 118, 125, 126, 127
Framlingham College 20, 21, 71, 191
France 23, 58–68, 75–128, 152–189
Freeman, Lance-Corporal 64, 65
Frost, Major J. D. 61, 63, 64, 66, 68
Fry, Flight Sergeant 113

George VI, King 69–71
Gibraltar 117
Glasgow 117
Glisy 161
Gneisnau 53, 56, 57
Gotha 43
Gravely 76
Gray, Lieutenant A. 175
Gray, Flight Lieutenant 112, 113
Greenhill, Flying Officer 54
Gunn, Squadron Leader 82, 83

Halifax, Lord 73, 74
Hamburg 43, 57, 76
Hanafin, Flight Lieutenant Tich 160
Hanigan, Sergeant 39
Harley, Flight Lieutenant 107, 111, 114
Hanover 76
Harborow, Flying Officer 113
Hardwicke, Sir Cedric 31, 32, 69
Hardwicke, Lady (Helena) 20, 31, 32, 51, 69
Harniman, Sergeant 39
Havilland, Sir Geoffrey de 130, 131
Hill, Flight Lieutenant Tony 59
Hitler, Adolf 22, 35, 37, 141
Hodges Air Chief Marshal Sir Lewis 77, 98, 99, 106, 107, 108, 109, 110, 114, 115, 119

Hodgkin, Dorothy, *see* Pickard, Dorothy
Hodgkin, Elsie 28, 30
Hodgkin, Harry 28, 29, 30
Hodgkin, Hilary 29, 50
Hodgkinson, Flying Officer 86
Holland 58, 59, 75, 82, 83
Holland, Admiral 54
Holland, Michel 135, 137, 139
Holleville, Maurice 145, 146
Home Guard 35, 36
Hood 52, 54, 55, 56
Hooper, Flight Lieutenant Robin 106, 107, 114, 115
Howard, Lee 149, 154, 157, 158, 172
Hunsdon, RAF 149, 152, 153, 161, 171, 195
Huntingdon 80

Iredale, Wing Commander Bob 158, 161, 171, 172, 176
Issoudun 90
Italy 43

Kahn, Harold 51
Kampen 83
Kattegat 54
Kenya 21, 22, 23, 24, 44, 46, 190
Khan, Noor Inayat 116, 120, 123
Kieffer, Hans 121, 122
King George V 55
Kirkman, R. 71
Krol, Wing Commander S. 77

La Presbytere 63
Lefort, Cecily 120, 124
Le Havre, 59, 101
Leigh, Vera 123
Leigh-Mallory, Air Chief Marshal Sir Trafford 150, 151
Le Mans 118
Lenglet, M. 166
Levin, Ian 194
Lille 81, 144
Lissett 119, 129

Loire, River 82, 94, 99, 120
London 17, 24, 30, 31, 52, 113, 194
Londonderry, Lord 134, 187, 188, 190
Lyneham 135
Lynn, Vera 42

McBride, Flying Officer 107, 110, 111
McCairns, Pilot Officer 42
McMaster, Flying Officer 113, 114
McRitchie, Squadron Leader 172, 176
Mannheim 57
Mans, Dr Antonin 164, 165, 166, 167, 168, 169, 170, 171
Marandellas 191
Marseilles 23, 96, 97, 117, 118
Martin, Monseigneur 170
Massigli, René, 91
Mediterranean 23
Medmenham 59, 136, 137, 140
Merifield, Squadron Leader J. R. H. 136
Mills, Sergeant 39
Ming 38, 39, 40, 41, 42, 57, 87, 101, 119, 134, 185, 186, 190–5
Moisan, Henri 161, 164
Molliens 173, 175
Mombasa 21, 45
Morris, Flight Sergeant 112, 114
Mountbatten, Lord 104
Munster 57

Naismith Shaw, Courtley 80, 81
Nearne, Eileen 124
Nesbitt-Dufort, Wing Commander John 91
Netheravon 62
Newmarket 38, 43
Nile, River 23
Norman, Gilbert 121, 123
Norman, Captain Sir Nigel 64
North Africa 24
North Sea 39
Norway 37, 38, 43, 53, 75

Olschanesky, Sonia 123
Operation Jericho 150–189
Orleans 90, 117
Overton-Fuller, Jean 121

Palestine 61
Paris 81, 117, 118, 120, 126, 144
Peenemunde Raid 135, 136, 137
Pepe 143, 144, 145
Perth 25, 26
Photographic Reconnaissance Unit 53, 54, 59, 136, 140
Pickard, Charles Percy 'Freddie'
  childhood 17–19; schooling 20–1; in Africa 21–24; training 25–28; marriage 29–34; with Ming 38, 40, 41, 42, 186–9, 190–5; with 99 Squadron 38–43; with 311 Squadron 43–52; in *Target for Tonight* 51, 52, 61, 69; with 9 Squadron 52–8; in *Prinz Eugen* Search 56; with 51 Squadron 58–68; in Bruneval Raid 58–68; with Royal Family 69–71; at Tempsford for SOE 75–105; birth of son 89; promoted Group Captain 106, 119; at Lissett 129; acquaintance with Déricourt 118–9, 127; Peenemunde Raid 137–141; in the Amiens Prison Raid 142–189; death 173–189
Pickard, Dorothy 28, 29, 30, 31, 32, 40, 41, 42, 50, 51, 52, 57, 87, 88, 89, 90, 101, 117, 118, 129, 130, 175, 185, 186, 187, 188, 189, 190–95
Pickard, George 126
Pickard, Helena *see* Hardwicke, Lady
Pickard, Marjorie 32, 69
Pickard, Mrs 18, 24, 69
Pickard, Nancy 17, 18, 19, 27, 69
Pickard, Nick 89, 101, 119, 134, 187, 190, 191
Pickard, Percy 69
Plewman, Eliane 123

Index

Plymouth 68
Poitiers 106, 118
Poland 77
Ponchardier, Dominique 143, 144, 145, 146, 147, 148, 153
Ponchardier, Pierre 143, 144, 146
Porthcawl 34
Predannack 91, 134
Priestley, J. B. 42
Prince of Wales 54
Prinz Eugen 52, 53, 55, 56, 57
Prosper network 118, 120, 121, 123, 125
Putt, Flight Lieutenant 99, 100, 105

Raeder, Grand-Admiral 53
Ravensbruck 123, 124
Red Sea 45
Regnault, Odile 168, 169
Rhodesia 190
Rhone, River 95
Riviere 143, 146
Robinson, Mr 20
Rodney 55
Rolfe, Lilian 124
Rommel, Field Marshal Erwin 58
Ross, Captain John 67
Rowden, Diana 120, 123
Rubech, Robert 137
Rudellat, Mme 124, 125
Ruhr 39, 43, 76
Rymills, Flying Officer 92, 93

St Eval 53, 85
St Gratien 173, 174, 175, 181
St Nazaire 58
St Quentin 145
St Valery 142
Salisbury 191
Salisbury Hall 149, 194
Sampson, Flight Lieutenant R. W. 172, 173, 176
Sandhurst 61
Sansom, Odette *see* Churchill
Savigny, G. S. 183

Scharnhorst 53, 56, 57
Scotland 25, 26, 64
Sculthorpe, RAF 130 132 186
Sellier, Louis 163
Serge 145
Shine, Pilot Officer 113
Simon, Sir John 33
Smith, J. A. 184
Snajdr, Flight Lieutenant Joe 48, 49, 50
SOE (Special Operations Executive) 74–128, 194
Somme, River 142, 150, 159, 165
Spanish Civil War 143
Spilsby 112
Squadrons:
  No. 9 52, 57
  No. 21 150, 156, 160, 171, 172
  No. 22 53
  No. 51 58–68
  No. 70 (RFC) 59
  No. 74 (RFC) 21
  No. 99 38–43
  No. 138 76, 77, 80
  No. 161 76, 77, 81, 89, 92, 105, 106, 116, 119, 122
  No. 198 159
  No. 311 (Czech) 43–52
  No. 464 (RAAF) 150, 156, 161, 171
  No. 487 (RNZAF) 150, 156, 161, 171
  No. 540 136
  No. 541 136
Stallbridge, Lord 34
Stewart, Corporal 64, 65
Storey, Sergeant 65
Stormy Down 34
Stradishall 76
Suckling, Pilot Officer Michael 54
Suez 45
Suffolk 55
Sugden, Squadron Leader Dick 158, 159, 172, 176
Suhren, Fritz 124
Suttill, Major Francis 120, 121, 123
Syria 117

Szabo, Violette 124

Tangmere 82, 85, 91, 96, 99, 107, 109
Target for To-night 51, 52, 61, 69, 105, 134, 136
Tassigny, Gen de Lattre de 96
Taylor, Pilot Oficer 94, 99, 105
Tempez, Captain 166, 170
Tempsford, RAF 74–119, 142
Thetford 46, 47
Thomas, Flying Officer 113
Thomas, Wing Commander Yeo 76, 78
Thruxton 64
Timothy, Lieutenant John 63, 65
Toman, Wing Commander 46, 47
Torquay 50
Tours 118, 120
Tovey, Admiral Sir John 54
Treport 139, 159
Tunis 77

Upper Heyford 33
Uxbridge 28

Verity, Squadron Leader Hugh 92, 93, 120, 121
Vernon, Captain Dennis 62, 63, 66
Victory 68

Wagland, Squadron Leader 107, 108
Wales 34
Watt, Harry 51
Westhampnett 150
Wick 53, 54
Wickham, Tony 149, 154, 157, 158, 172
Wilhelmshaven 43
Wittering, RAF 28, 44, 46, 47, 52
Woodbridge 109, 112, 113

Young Lieutenant Peter 63, 67